Colleges of the Forgotten Americans

Colleges of the Forgotten Americans

A PROFILE OF STATE COLLEGES AND
REGIONAL UNIVERSITIES

by *E. Alden Dunham*

Executive Associate, Carnegie Corporation of New York

with a commentary by *David Riesman*

Second of a Series of Profiles Sponsored by
The Carnegie Commission on Higher Education

MC GRAW-HILL BOOK COMPANY
New York   St. Louis   San Francisco   London
Sydney   Toronto   Mexico   Panama

The Carnegie Commission on Higher Education,
1947 Center Street, Berkeley, California 94704,
has sponsored preparation of this Profile as a
part of a continuing effort to present significant
information and issues for public discussion.
The views expressed are those of the author.

COLLEGES OF THE FORGOTTEN AMERICANS
A Profile of State Colleges and Regional Universities

" . . . the great majority of Americans, the forgotten Americans—the nonshouters, the nondemonstrators. . . . They are good people, they are decent people; they work, and they save, and they pay their taxes, and they care."

RICHARD M. NIXON

"If we could first know where we are, and whither we are tending, we could then better judge what to do, and how to do it."

ABRAHAM LINCOLN

"Someday we'll play in the Rose Bowl."

STATE COLLEGE OFFICIAL

Foreword

The state colleges and regional universities are America's most restless institutions of higher learning. Their history spans less than 150 years, but during that time they have, typically, played four changing roles: as post-high school academies, as normal schools devoted solely to the education of teachers, as four-year liberal arts colleges with strong technical emphases in teacher education, industrial arts, and home economics, and as comprehensive colleges giving also professional education in engineering and business administration and graduate work at the M.A. level. Some have become regional universities with research programs and Ph.D. degrees. And there still remains an unsettled quality about their functions, standards, offerings, faculties, and clientele. They continue to seek a brighter place in the academic sun.

These 279 colleges and universities now enroll about one-fifth of all college students, and this proportion will continue to rise. They also produce almost half of the nation's teachers. This is not only an important but also a neglected segment of higher education—neglected by the press, the public, and state legislatures alike. But it is not neglected by Mr. Dunham. He gives us the first good account—full of first-hand personal impressions—of these important institutions of American higher education.

But what will be their future? Mr. Dunham suggests that they may have a special role to play in training for the doctor of arts degree—a nonresearch teaching degree of high prestige.

This is the second of several profiles of higher education—the first is by Andrew Greeley on the Catholic colleges—to be issued by the Carnegie Commission on Higher Education as a contribution to a better understanding of the diversity in American institutions of higher learning.

Clark Kerr
Chairman
The Carnegie Commission
on Higher Education

July, 1969

$\mathcal{C}$ontents

Introduction

This project, along with a number of others similar to it, was undertaken at the request of the Carnegie Commission on Higher Education in an effort to put together a kind of map of higher education. Each of several authors was to describe the features of his institutions, including their history, structure, functions, governance, financing, students and faculty, and curricula, as well as problems and aspirations.

My assignment was to take a look at four-year state colleges and what are sometimes known as regional universities, basically the membership of the American Association of State Colleges and Universities (AASCU) (see Appendix A). This association in early 1968 had 231 institutional members in 44 states plus Guam, the District of Columbia, and the Virgin Islands. When so-called nonmembers (see Appendix B)—places that don't pay dues but are on the AASCU mailing list—are added to the list, the number goes to 279, and that becomes the magic figure for my purpose. These 210 colleges and 69 universities represent over 10 percent of the country's higher educational institutions and enroll 21 percent of all students in higher education. This enrollment of 1 in 5 college students today will be 1 in 4 tomorrow and 1 in 3 the day after tomorrow. These places are growing very rapidly; they are important and deserve more attention then they get.

My assignment also included municipally governed four-year institutions. Here a striking change has occurred within the past few years. Largely because of financial strains at the local level, municipal institutions have been transformed into state colleges and universities. Many have been taken over completely; others are something of a hybrid. The University of Cincinnati, for example, is "municipally sponsored, state affiliated," with five board members appointed by the mayor and four by the governor. The

City University of New York is the only major completely municipally controlled institution left, and half of CUNY's budget now comes from New York State. I should emphasize that I am referring to baccalaureate institutions, not to two-year community colleges, of which there are large numbers under municipal control.

The story of the state colleges and regional universities is an absorbing one, and I hope in this Profile to capture some of the fascination, excitement, and problems of these institutions. All publicly financed and controlled, many of them until fairly recently have been relatively sleepy, single-purpose, teacher training colleges. Having acquired a taste for higher status and strong ambitions, they are at various stages of movement along a spectrum from their single-purpose origins as teachers colleges toward multipurpose university status and prestige. Emerging colleges, developing colleges—different descriptions are used.

The term *state college* has no mystery about it, but *regional university* needs some definition. All states have at least one landgrant institution, and many have separate state universities— Michigan State University and the University of Michigan, for example. Both these institutions have statewide constituencies. Eastern Michigan University, Northern Michigan University, Central Michigan University, and Western Michigan University have names that reflect their regional concern, and they are dubbed *regional universities*—a term some of these places find too binding in relation to their ambitions.

Slippery Rock is a state college in Pennsylvania, not a joke dreamed up by sportswriters in football season. Assiduously avoiding troublesome campuses, President Nixon scheduled a June, 1969, speech at General Beadle State College in South Dakota, where the students—the sons and daughters of the President's constituency—take a dim view of protesters. Former President Johnson graduated from Southwest Texas State College, and I am surprised that not more was made of two state colleges in Vermont—Lyndon and Johnson! Though I did not have a chance to travel to either Texas or Vermont, during the late spring of 1968 I did visit a number of state colleges and regional universities. Warm hospitality was extended to me on 14 campuses: California State College at Los Angeles, California; Chico State College, Chico, California; Ball State University, Muncie, Indiana; University of Northern Iowa, Cedar Falls, Iowa; Kansas State College of Pittsburg, Kansas; Kansas State Teachers College, Emporia,

Kansas; Western Michigan University, Kalamazoo, Michigan; Missouri Southern College, Joplin, Missouri; Trenton State College, Trenton, New Jersey; City College of New York, New York City, New York; State University at Albany, New York; State University College at Brockport, New York; East Carolina University, Greenville, North Carolina; Federal City College, Washington, D.C.

I visited these 14 campuses on the basis of whim, plane schedules, and advice. I deliberately avoided weak institutions but did try to see different kinds of places. My procedure was to call the president and request a schedule that usually included an hour or so with him, a session with an academic dean or vice-president, another session with the dean or chairman of the education department, a meeting with a group of six or so faculty members, who were often members of the faculty senate or equivalent body, and a meeting with a small group of students, usually from student government or the campus newspaper. (By the way, on most campuses I scheduled an appointment with the best tennis player available and, amazingly, emerged with a winning season!)

The visits usually were for a day only, and my impressions were bound to be superficial. Yet my goal was simply to soak up the atmosphere of the campus and to get at some of the bigger issues bothering administrators, faculty, and students. Arriving in town the evening before my visit, I would read catalogs, reports, and student newspapers. That evening or the next day between appointments I would spend considerable time wandering around the campus—in and out of dormitories, the library, the gymnasium, the student union. I spent time reading notices on bulletin boards and chatting informally with students and faculty in the library or cafeteria. The coffee was often very good, and the thick shakes superb! During my perambulations I ran into everything from concerts and heated black power discussions to a session a group of girls were having with a wig salesman. The evening after my visit was generally spent talking into a dictaphone in an attempt to freeze some of the fleeting impressions of the day just past. My children were delighted with the T-shirts I bought for them on sale at several campuses. The reason for the discount: the campus stores often had a difficult time keeping the insignia on the shirt current with the rapidly changing names of the institutions.

In addition to these 14 site visits, I spent time either interviewing or corresponding with a number of people directly concerned with these institutions at the state level. This statewide perspective is important because of the growing trend toward coordinating councils and other boards responsible for the efficient use of state money in the development of higher education. I also corresponded with the presidents of a number of institutions I did not have a chance to visit and exchanged letters as well with a considerable number of knowledgeable people whose wisdom and advice proved most helpful.

I should note that my personal interest in state colleges and regional universities is not new. As a staff member on James B. Conant's study of teacher education a few years ago, I had the opportunity to visit several of these institutions. Also, my work with Carnegie Corporation of New York has taken me on visits to state colleges. And though I have never held a position in one, I am an alumnus—two summer courses at Montclair State College many years ago. (These were English literature courses unavailable at Harvard the preceding year!)

Colleges of the Forgotten Americans

1. To Frame the Target: Three Studies

In a nutshell, the most salient characteristics of state colleges and regional universities are rapid change of function and astounding growth. Many are quickly moving along a spectrum from single-purpose teachers colleges to multipurpose universities. One of the ironies of this movement is that a first-class teachers college may become a third-class university as it grows and changes its function.

The State University at Albany has moved farthest toward full university status of any of the institutions I visited. It is at the far right of the spectrum. At the far left is Trenton State College, which, along with the other five state colleges in New Jersey, is just barely emerging beyond the teachers college tradition. At about the same location along the spectrum are the two Kansas colleges, as well as Missouri Southern, which is a brand-new college trying to blossom immediately as a multipurpose institution offering both liberal arts and applied programs. I would place the State University College at Brockport somewhere to the right of the center of this spectrum as a place which until very recently would have been no further along than Trenton but which has made considerable changes in the past very few years. Moving along still further are the University of Northern Iowa and Ball State University. At about the same spot, I would place the two California state colleges, Cal State at Los Angeles and Chico State, as well as East Carolina University. Then comes Western Michigan University, which is still far short of Albany in some aspects of development. Because of its unusual tradition, City College of New York is a special case and must be treated differently. The same is true of Federal City College.

A brief description of three institutions located at different points along the spectrum might be useful as a way to begin digging into what these institutions are all about and to make the discussions in later sections more relevant. Near the far left is Kansas State Teachers College; at the center, State University College at Brockport; toward the right, Western Michigan University.

KANSAS STATE TEACHERS COLLEGE AT EMPORIA

Emporia is midway between Kansas City and Wichita and is probably best known as the home of William Allen White and the *Emporia Gazette.* For an Easterner driving to Emporia through the rolling countryside, there arises an image of a bygone era. Indeed, it seems appropriate that Kansas State Teachers College at Emporia is the last state teachers college in the nation. Its name is unique.

There is nothing very quaint about the business section of the town, population 20,000, but the residential area has a peculiar charm with its red-brick streets and white clapboard houses. William Allen White actually attended Emporia College, a struggling private liberal arts school, though the teachers college has much of his library.

I arrived at the campus just as the summer session was beginning. Normally, some 7,000 students are somewhat jammed together on a 200-acre campus with red-brick architecture of rather ancient vintage. At most other campuses construction abounds everywhere, but not at Emporia. New buildings are needed; the situation is desperate. A couple of buildings have been condemned. Nevertheless, the prevailing impression of the campus is pleasant and inviting; there is even a small lake at its center.

Perhaps its hallmark is the overall friendliness—not uncommon at institutions of this kind but very unfamiliar to one who has spent time at more prestigious, faster-paced places. At Emporia, no snarling policeman accosted me as I tried to park. Instead, a fellow came up, introduced himself, and shook my hand! The bright Kansas sunshine, tall stately trees shading the old buildings, elderly elementary school marms with below-the-knee flowered print dresses passing between classes—the pleasant scene was seemingly devoid of the tensions gripping higher education generally.

However, beneath the surface there are many tensions at Kansas State Teachers College. These have to do with the mission and purpose of the place. Like so many similar institutions, this one began as a normal school, "the exclusive purposes of which shall be the instruction of persons, both male and female, in the art of teaching." To this day, the primary purpose has been to train teachers for Kansas schools — at first for the elementary schools and later, when secondary education itself became "common," for the high schools as well.

The town took great pride in "The Normal," although there were many problems over the years. The third president, in particular, had a very rough time. A grasshopper invasion cut incomes to such an extent that faculty salaries suffered badly; the main building was burned; the state legislature refused to appropriate more funds; a man selling college land embezzled money; a tornado struck the campus (the president himself made the repairs); and finally a fire completely destroyed the building, including all the equipment and the personal possessions of the president. The following summer he was fired!

By 1890, Kansas State Normal at Emporia was reported to be the largest state normal school in the nation. In 1923, "The Normal" became Kansas State Teachers College at Emporia. For many years it had ceased to be simply a secondary school preparing young rural women to teach in the elementary schools; it had become a college, and the name change seemed appropriate. In 1928, the North Central Association admitted the college to membership in the university and college division, a step upward on the ladder of academic respectability. The master's degree in education was authorized in 1929, and in 1931 the college was authorized to offer a nonteaching B.A. degree. But over the years the preparation of teachers has been by far the overriding concern at Emporia. Only now is there real debate over the mission of the place and, consequently, over the *teachers college* name. Should the institution expand its programs, change its name, and thereby follow the example of dozens of other institutions like it in tradition and role?

But before highlighting the current debate, let's take a look at what the place is like now. At the undergraduate level the enrollment is about 6,000, having multiplied many times over under the enthusiastic leadership of the former president, John King, a professional educator who believed strongly in teacher education and cemented relationships with public school districts throughout Kansas. John Visser, his successor, sees a maximal growth to about 10,000 students toward the end of the century. This is in sharp contrast to projections of many state colleges where population pressures are surging. Kansas is just not that populous a state. Moreover, President Visser feels that a college of less than 10,000 students is large enough to maintain quality programs and sufficient scope but still small enough to retain institutional identity and solidarity. In any case, the dormitory shortage is such that only 15 percent of the students at present can be housed on campus, and Emporia is not large enough to absorb many more through boarding arrangements.

The undergraduates are like teacher education students everywhere—only more so. For generations, schoolteaching has been, especially for girls, a way for socioeconomic advancement. In any institution which prepares the majority of its students for teaching, the students are, for the most part, from lower-middle-class backgrounds and are often first-generation collegians. The straight liberal arts program has little appeal to parents who, not having been to college themselves, want to see a salable product after four years. For this reason, many boys head for engineering or business; girls have traditionally chosen teaching as a respectable position in lieu of marriage. The current ratio of men to women in all higher education is about 3 to 2; it is not surprising at Emporia to find as many women as men.

As a group, the students tend to be apathetic about national issues and politically conservative—very definitely not in the mold of the New Left protest generation. Demonstrations are still limited to panty raids. Still, there is a small activist group, and the president of the student body for the past two years has been a Negro. There are some 200 to 300 Negroes on the campus.

Student power is not yet an issue. There are probably two reasons for this. These are not affluent students, like many of those protesting elsewhere; college means a financial sacrifice to them and their families, and many of them must work in order to stay in college. Tuition, room and board, books, and other expenses cost over $1,700 annually. But the second reason has to do with the nature of the institution itself. This is not a cold, impersonal place; students are not IBM numbers. It is a teaching institution, and the faculty are concerned about individual students. Indeed, students say that the faculty tend to mark entirely too softly and do not flunk out enough people who enter under the open-door admissions policy in Kansas, whereby any high school graduate can gain admission to any state institution. This softness is attributed in part to the pervading influence of professional educators, including the former president, who apparently went out of his way to keep woefully weak students around the campus. Evidence of his humanitarian instincts is seen in various forms, including special ramps built for handicapped students, for whom the teachers college has a special concern.

About 70 percent of last year's 1,000 graduates were prepared to teach, and a great bulk of these in fact entered teaching, dispersing themselves generally about the state of Kansas. Both elementary and secondary teachers are prepared. Enrolled at the master's degree level are 1,000 students, just about all of them in-service teachers taking evening, Saturday morning, and summer programs to keep up with their fields—and to move up on the salary schedule. (I suspect one of the main reasons for heavy attendance at summer sessions is simply the desire of adults to talk with other adults in a relaxed fashion without children around. One of the most interesting people I met was a nun who was principal of a *public* elementary school in western Kansas.)

Not many people realize that up until just a few years ago the majority of elementary school teachers in the United States did not have bachelor's degrees. One of the major programs in the former teachers colleges, including Kansas State Teachers College, involved extension work throughout rural areas, in particular, to bring two-year normal school graduates up to the baccalaureate level. This job has been pretty much completed, with the result that at Emporia the extension business is not as large as it once was.

As one might expect, the academic organization of the institution has paralleled public school teacher certification. There are a number of departments or divisions: art, biology, business, education, English, foreign language, health and physical education, recreation and athletics, home economics, industrial art, library science, mathematics, music, physical science, psychology, social science, and speech. Note that biology is a separate department and indeed one of the strongest, while physics and chemistry are subsumed under physical science—an arrangement reflecting traditional demands for secondary school teachers. Even today in Kansas there are probably few full-time physics teachers, ones who do not have to teach chemistry and perhaps some mathematics as well. Yet there probably are large numbers of full-time biology teachers simply because of the much heavier enrollments in biology.

More revealing is the case in the social sciences. Traditional secondary schools simply don't have courses in economics, political science, sociology, or anthropology. Basically, what is taught is history with a smattering of these other disciplines sometimes thrown in. The result for teacher education is a department of social science without full-fledged majors in any of the disciplines. The relevance of the other departments to the organization of the public schools seems clear. This traditional academic structure in a teachers college is very much under question and is one of the first things to change when an institution expands its program.

Until a year ago, the president operated with a dean of the graduate division and a dean of instruction plus a fiscal officer and a few men with the title of director. For a small, cozy institution, this kind of administration was appropriate. There are strains now, with 6,000 students severely overcrowding both the facilities and the programs. A new administrative plan is in the works.

What's In a Name? Let's return to the debate over the function of the college and its name. Two similar colleges in Kansas are now called *state colleges,* reflecting a deliberate attempt to increase both the liberal arts phase of their programs and the breadth of their nonteaching majors. Attempts are made through applied programs at Kansas State College of Pittsburg, for example, to relate to the immediate region in areas other than public education. Some faculty at Emporia want to move in this direction and feel, moreover, that the phrase *teachers college* carries with it connotations of mediocrity, especially since Sputnik. This means problems with faculty recruitment and, perhaps, with student recruitment. (But added to the problems of faculty recruitment caused by the name of the institution is the dismal salary schedule: C on the scale of the American Association of University Professors (AAUP). This low salary schedule also helps to explain why only about 30 percent of the faculty have doctor's degrees. This place and many others like it simply cannot afford to hire very many experienced people with reputations and must settle for the inexperienced at low rates.)

The name also implies a vocational thrust, which some of the faculty on the academic side dislike. This group has high hopes that the new president, with a Ph.D. in history, will change both the image and the substance of the place. As one professor in secondary education said in referring to his colleague in biology, "When Helen goes to her national conventions, there is a stigma when she says she is from a teachers college, but there is none when I go to my conventions." Since the liberal arts base of teacher education programs generally throughout the country has been considerably strengthened over the years, and Emporia is no exception, the academic people servicing the general education programs are larger in number and louder in voice when it comes to matters of this kind.

But why hasn't this teachers college gone the route of all others in the nation? The answer apparently lies in the conviction of the former president and a few influential faculty members that the road to prosperity is straight ahead and not at a right angle. The institution has developed a name and a constituency for itself; its region is statewide and not confined to its immediate neighborhood, which is sparsely populated to begin with and yet surrounded by larger universities. There are many community colleges and private liberal arts colleges as well. To drop the name and change the game would mean a loss in distinctiveness. The broad political base of support in the form of public school people throughout the state is too important an asset to cast aside easily. The prime exponent of this point of view on the campus has been the chairman of the division of education, who has left for another post. What the future will hold remains to be seen. At the time of my visit there was a long-range planning committee at work on the problem.

I talked with an impressive group of students, who spoke knowledgeably about the institution. In fact, a student committee on the mission of the place took a look at other colleges. Their conclusion apparently had little to do with the name but rather with the improvement of things in general. They pointed out that faculty salaries were the worst in the state, while the student-teacher ratio was the highest. Through the efforts of one faculty member in particular, there had been some research money from various sources, but only a trickle. Students with whom I spoke would like to see the institution keep its present name but drastically improve the quality of its programs. This feeling seemed to coincide with the views of at least some of the faculty with whom I spoke. What this generality means when it comes to specifics is yet another question. In other institutions, improvement in quality means, in very traditional terms, more Ph.D.'s on the faculty doing more research and, generally, paying less attention to undergraduate teaching—the very thing the students are worried about.

Kansas State Teachers College at Emporia can very well stand as a symbol of the quandary faced by all the developing institutions: it has to make a decision about its role. Among the institutions

I saw, this one is not further along in development than Trenton State College in New Jersey with respect to current mission, programs, faculty, and organization. But should it move further along the spectrum? Perhaps it can make whatever changes it wants without changing its name, and it may well be that a reputation as the last institution of a particular kind is very much of an asset.

However, the relationship to the state is important, and the regents may prefer to see the state's resources in higher education deployed differently, strengthening the state system by not concentrating so heavy a bulk of teacher education at Emporia. In short, what may be the college's self-interest in preserving the political base with the public schools may not be compatible with the interest of the state as a whole. In any event, it is an interesting situation. This is a friendly place now, warm and cohesive; I suspect there are less placid days ahead.

STATE UNIVERSITY COLLEGE AT BROCKPORT, NEW YORK

If Kansas State Teachers College at Emporia is a locomotive still sitting at the station building up steam, Brockport has its throttle wide open and is speeding down the track. Like most Eastern teachers colleges, it ran way behind schedule, but in the past two or three years it has made up much of its lost time. Or, to go back to the original image of the spectrum, Brockport has moved recently from a position on the far left, along with places like Trenton and Emporia, to at least a middle position, maybe beyond. This rapid development has been made possible by Brockport's place within the prospering State University of New York (SUNY) system. The system now comprises 67 colleges and centers. Fifty-seven of these conduct classes, including four university centers, two medical centers, seven specialized colleges, six two-year agricultural and technical colleges, twenty-eight locally sponsored, two-year community colleges, and ten colleges of arts and science (Brockport is an example). Three additional state colleges are being developed, two of them in Nassau and Westchester counties and a third to be located near Utica.

Several jets a day fly nonstop from New York to Rochester, from where Brockport lies about 15 miles west along the shore of Lake Ontario. Rochester itself is a thriving city, the third largest in New York State, and Monroe County in which both it and Brockport are located is purported to be one of the wealthiest counties in the state. Industries such as Eastman Kodak, Xerox, Taylor

Instruments, and Bausch and Lomb are prospering and attracting many new people to the area. Educational expectations are increasing rapidly, and this places a heavy burden upon the existing institutions. The best known is the University of Rochester. In addition, there are a number of community colleges. Buffalo, about 1½ hours' drive away, has both a major university center and a state college within the SUNY system. The thriving metropolis in and around Rochester has only State University College at Brockport.

The village of Brockport itself has only recently begun to be touched by the fast tempo of modern life. At the core of the village are old wooden-frame houses dating back at least to the turn of the century. But at the periphery, developments of small houses rather chaotically placed are spreading, with the inevitable big shopping plazas complete with acres of macadam parking lots. Once the expressway system links Brockport with Rochester, the entire village will take on a different flavor. Both town and gown are changing.

The first building one sees when approaching the campus is a large red-brick structure with STATE TEACHERS COLLEGE etched in concrete across the entrance. This building and an old white-frame Victorian antique, which used to be the president's house and now serves as a faculty dining room, are the only tangible ties with the past. What has taken place in the past two or three years is "instant" campus, and it looks as though not one but several bombs had hit it. There are holes in the ground everywhere, bulldozers moving earth here and there, and buildings going up in every direction. The northern section of the campus is packed with new buildings—red-brick modern, of course. The architecture is unimpressive, largely because the buildings look alike and are crowded together. The addition of landscaping may help considerably. Also, the campus is long and narrow, which does not lend itself to coherence. But there is a large tract of land across a Penn-Central freight line that will provide more room for expansion and undoubtedly a more pleasing environment.

The building program has been fantastic, some $45 million for science, general classrooms, infirmary, communications, fine arts, physical education, administration, student union, dining halls, and dormitories (including four high-rise dorms, in one of which a colleague and I stayed). The old union building will become a computer-math center. The new library will enable a jump from the current 150,000 volumes to 350,000 volumes. Other facilities include a fine-looking laboratory school as well as a 500-acre area about 8 miles away that is used for activities such as conferences, picnics, and boating.

With all this new construction and indeed with what amounts to a brand-new faculty and student body within the past three years, one has a sense of a lack of tradition. There is a coldness about the buildings which time will undoubtedly take care of. The high-rise men's dormitory in which we stayed consisted of three-bedroom suites with a living room and bath. With the new linoleum floors, sparkling tile, and white walls, there was an antiseptic cast about the place. Atmosphere was provided by the students, who set up a loud hi-fi blaring forth rock and roll music through the ventilating system. This was rather unique. Every room received the full benefit. So did the rest of the campus, since the music issued forth from the open vents on the roof!

The place began as a Baptist "college" in the 1830s and had difficulties right from the start. It became a secondary school for a while, and then, in 1866, the people of Brockport were successful in their fight to locate one of the newly created normal schools in their village. In 1867, the Brockport State Normal School came into being. "The Normal" prepared teachers for elementary schools while still serving as the local high school. By the mid-1930s the normal school era was clearly coming to an end. Consideration was given to closing Brockport entirely, plagued as it was by the depression and obsolescent buildings. But the enterprising principal at that time saved the school by bringing in federal funds for a new building (much against the better judgment of the rock-ribbed Republican villagers). He enrolled the wives of faculty members as students in order to meet the minimum enrollment figure of 300 as established by the state legislature!

In 1942, New York's normal schools became degree-granting state teachers colleges. In 1948, SUNY was created, and again the name changed, this time to State University Teachers College. In 1952, it became the State University College of Education. During this time no new stationery was printed since nobody knew what the name of the place was to become. The only certainty was that the institution's function was to prepare teachers.

In 1962, additional functions were added, and the name changed once more—this time to the State University College of Arts and Sciences, the present full title. With the new general-purpose mission went authorization to develop curricula for the

A.B. degree. The first M.A. degree awarded in a field other than education was conferred in English in June, 1969. A number of other master's degree programs are to follow. At the present time there are no doctoral programs nor indications of any in the offing. Other than education, there are no professional schools either, though Albert Brown, the new and very energetic president, has his eye on a law school as something badly needed in the Rochester area.

The Transformation of a Teachers College

It is important to realize that as recently as 1948 New York State had no system of higher education aside from a series of teachers colleges. The motto of SUNY is "Let each become all he is capable of being." Though aimed at students, this could well be the motto of the state colleges, for it surely reflects the mood at Brockport. It is an ambitious and enterprising place. President Brown came to Brockport from Eastern Michigan University, where he was dean of the college. In just two years he has turned this institution on its end. And he has done it apparently without alienating the old guard faculty. The contrast before and after is startling.

Though some progress had been made toward the introduction of a broader curriculum, Brockport remained, until 1965, very much a single-purpose, teacher training institution. Its legacy from the normal school days was the training of elementary school teachers, and its other main business was training physical education teachers. This meant that there was no true upper-division academic work. This is a vital fact to remember when one talks about transforming a teachers college into a college of arts and science. Elementary teacher training consists largely of professional education courses with a spread of lower-division general education courses designed to enable the elementary teachers to teach just about anything to young children. Typically, a program for elementary teachers is mostly breadth with little academic depth. The physical education program at Brockport was even more devoid of academic content. President Brown says Brockport was fully a decade behind Eastern Michigan University, from which he had just come.

The Brockport faculty had been organized into three divisions, sarcastically referred to by some as "the Trinity." These were education, physical education, and liberal studies—the latter representing the Holy Spirit, a presence that was somehow sensed but not really manifest. There was, according to one older faculty member, "lip service to quality education and academic disciplines, but little understanding of what was required to have *both* breadth and depth." So the goal became to introduce true upper-division academic work—in short, academic majors. Now, even elementary teachers must take an academic major.

To accomplish the task, many of the faculty recognized the necessity for a drastic overhaul of the academic organization and programs, as well as for an input of new faculty members. Fortunately for President Brown, he arrived on the scene just when enrollments were beginning to skyrocket. Thus, he could hire large numbers of new faculty, and he concentrated upon top academic people at the senior ranks who would teach upper-division and graduate-level courses. The Trinity was dissolved, and in its place six different faculties, each with a number of new departments, were created. This meant that faculty votes were spread around so that the education and physical education people no longer controlled policy. But the important matter was the infusion of senior faculty, many of them new department chairmen who then brought in people like themselves. In addition, the president established the rule that no faculty member would be hired unless his credentials were passed upon by the president's office. And the credentials for hiring very definitely included a good list of publications and a doctor's degree.

As for the departments, social science was divided into its component disciplines. Science was broken up into the usual components of chemistry, physics, biology, and geology. Also psychology, which had been linked with education, became a brand-new department within the science faculty. Interestingly, many of the old psychology types, who were in reality educationists with a smattering of psychology, stayed in education, so that the new psychology department is one of the "hardest" of the new departments in the sense that it focuses on rats and pigeons rather than on schoolchildren. (In one of the beginning psychology courses, each student has his rat and the student's grade depends not upon how well he does but upon how well the rat does!)

Traditionally, English was the strongest department because of its size and centrality to whatever did amount to liberal studies; moreover its chairman was a leader among the faculty. This meant that English was able to upgrade itself more rapidly than other departments, accounting for the fact that it was the first to receive authorization to proceed with a master's degree.

It is interesting that mathematics and the sciences were among the last departments to be affected by the new regime. This was due largely to the thin faculty market in these areas. With less change in the composition of faculty, some of these departments still feel more affinity toward the traditional role of teacher preparation than does, say, the English department. The psychology and geology departments are exceptions.

The sociology-anthropology department has a Chicago Ph.D. as chairman. There was no philosophy department to begin with, but this new department has moved about as far as any. In 1968, the International Philosophic Year program brought to the campus many of the most distinguished philosophers in the world. This has meant an understandable limelight position for Brockport.

The paternalism of the former administration has been toned down. It seems most of the power in the place once resided in the business office, since it was the business officer who in effect made educational policies through his budgetary decisions. Many amusing stories are told about the old operation. Apparently, there was one piano on the campus, which, ancient and decrepit as it was, finally broke down in the middle of a concert. The business officer agreed to purchase a new one, which he did, buying the cheapest Steinway he could find. He then proceeded to keep the piano locked in a cage where no one could have access to it. (One of the rules was that no jazz musician could play on it.) The former administration also took great delight and pride in turning back to the SUNY central office in Albany more money at the end of the year than any of the other institutions!

Faculty governance had little meaning at all. A story is told of one man who was asked about the committees under which the former president had operated. A particular committee was mentioned, and the man professed ignorance about it; he was then told that he had been the chairman of that committee for several years! In any case, with a total revision of the academic departmental structure came the introduction of a faculty senate, with a constitution and all that goes with it. This was an important move. In attracting stronger academic types to the institution, President Brown recognized clearly the necessity for giving this new breed a stronger voice in the governance of the place.

Generally, the faculty seemed satisfied with the development of the academic senate, although the new breed was a bit restive, not being able to serve on the senate until they had been on the campus for three years — an important device which ensured some control by older faculty members and some continuity, rather than a sharp and perhaps destructive break with the past. But a recent change accommodates newer faculty members. A few members of the new breed belong to the American Federation of Teachers, and there is some talk—nothing serious at this point—about organizing under the AFT. The faculty do not seem to chafe under their 12-hour teaching load, since apparently anyone with some research project or grant can get his load reduced without much trouble. But the faculty definitely feel the pressure to do research and to publish in order to be promoted.

One interesting footnote to the reorganization is the fact that the president and his key administrative officers placed on a blackboard just outside his office the layout of what the new organization might look like. They then invited all the faculty, over a period of time, to come in and, with a piece of chalk, mark up the plan in any way they thought desirable. The faculty literally had a hand in designing the structure.

There is no doubt that some people who have been in the institution for several years feel threatened. A new hardness has hit the place, with emphasis upon academic disciplines, research, competition, publication. Research funds have gone from $1,000 or so to $1 million in less than two years. Some of the women, in particular, feel insecure about all this change. But because of the enrollment increase the president did not have to get rid of faculty; he simply found other positions for several, and he has had many former opponents come forward within the past year to agree with him that his changes were for the best.

The very high salaries paid in the SUNY system also contributed to easing the transition for the old guard faculty. On the AAUP scale, full professors have B ratings, but all others are at the A level. At Brockport one man has been getting $25,000 for ten months, and many are getting $19,000. The full professors average about $16,000. The overall teacher-student ratio is about 1 to 14. The goal is 1 to 15 at the lower-division level, 1 to 12 at the upper-division level, and 1 to 10 at the master's level. Departmental chairmen apparently have fairly wide discretion in how they use their funds to work out their programs.

President Brown says emphatically that for real change to take place in an institution without ripping it apart, there must be considerable growth. In 1965, the total enrollment was about 2,500, with 200 faculty. Today it is 5,500, with 350 faculty.

Enrollment will continue to climb rapidly; an additional 98 faculty members were new to the campus in the fall of 1968. Fifty-four percent of the faculty have been at Brockport fewer than three years. Summarizing his program, President Brown says that the major problems were to identify the different goals for the institution—i.e., a multipurpose college—then to create a structure that would move toward those goals, and finally to find the right staff. About 57 percent of the faculty, most of them people hired within the past two years, now hold doctorates. The target is 66 percent by 1970.

It is quite clear that many of the new breed of faculty are at Brockport because of the lure, indeed the gamble, that Brockport will eventually become a university center within the SUNY system, an addition to the four currently in existence. The SUNY trustees have said *no* to doctoral programs at the state colleges, yet the faculty do not accept this answer as final. Their morale seems to be high and in sharp contrast to what I found in the California state college system.

Given the new thrust toward academic excellence, research, and nonteaching majors, what has happened to teacher education? The percentage of enrolled students prepared as teachers has dropped significantly from 100 percent just a few years ago to about 70 percent. At the same time, however, in absolute numbers there have been more teachers prepared, so that Brockport stands next to Buffalo as the chief producer of teachers in the state system.

Whether this increase at Brockport and at other former teachers colleges is sufficient to meet the demand for teachers is another question. One answer is that better teachers, indeed teachers who have more of a commitment to the profession and will stay in teaching, are being produced. Under the old teachers college regime large numbers of students, especially girls, were enrolled who really cared nothing for teaching but wanted some kind of job security, marriage, and the like. The percentage of students prepared to teach that actually enter the teaching profession has been only about 70 percent nationwide. President Brown and others are quite sure that a much higher percentage of Brockport graduates enter teaching as a career and stay there. Involved is the old argument about what one does in a time of shortage—lower or raise the standards to increase the supply. The people in teacher education generally, certainly at Brockport, take the latter position, though it is evident that school superintendents caught in a bind, as they have been for the past several years, hire almost anyone who comes along regardless of qualifications.

In short, Brockport officially claims no diminution of concern for teacher preparation, but it is obvious from talking to faculty that within the new breed there are large numbers who couldn't care less about preparing schoolteachers. The widely publicized gap between education professors and academic professors found on many university campuses is a problem that is barely beginning to rear its head on the Brockport campus.

Indeed, I tried without success to stir up a fight between the two points of view during a session with a group of faculty members. A couple of the old breed regretted the tremendous spurt in size of the place, feeling that impersonality and anonymity had begun to pervade the campus. This point of view is shared by many, especially by those traditionally concerned more with students than with their disciplines. One woman regretted the fact that elementary teachers now needed an academic major, feeling that their job required much more breadth than depth. But, aside from these two criticisms, all the faculty members with whom I spoke were unanimous in their praise of what was going on, the excitement of the place, its promise for the future.

Students and Programs

In the freshman class of 900, girls slightly outnumber boys—again, a reflection of the elementary teacher education tradition. Sixty percent of the class get some financial assistance (excluding the New York State Scholar incentive awards, which everyone receives) to meet the annual estimated budget of $1,800 to $2,000. About 40 percent of the freshman applicants are admitted, and just under half of the admitted group enroll in the fall. Test-score averages keep going up; the average freshman in 1968 had the equivalent of an SAT verbal score of 548.

At places like Emporia or the University of Northern Iowa, there appears to be a preponderance of corn-fed students from rural, Protestant backgrounds; at Brockport there is much more of a seasoning of city-bred Catholics and Jews. I suspect this is true of the faculty as well. Overall, the students at Brockport seem typical of teacher education students at most places—low-level on the socioeconomic ladder, vocationally oriented, conservative politically. One of the student government officers, a perfect organization man, stated flatly that students have a large role in the governance of the place, serving on all the important faculty committees and being taken into the counsel of the president when important issues are at hand. He doesn't see any need for a move toward student power or an enlargement of student activity. As for the apathy of the students in general, he and other students said that things have changed significantly in the past two years; a great difference is noted between the senior class and the current freshmen and sophomores. The latter are considered brighter and have wider outside interests. The students with whom I talked said that there is some drug use on the campus but probably very little.

Yet there is some agitation among the students, and a minority party has dedicated itself to a greater voice for students in governance. On a bulletin board ran the ad for the minority party:

Brockport State Is No Longer A *Little* Red School House. It Is Now A *Big* Red School House. Let's Work Together And Make It A University. Brockport State Is Changing—But Much Of The Change Is Chaotic and Unplanned. . . . What Do We Want? A Student Voice In The Academic Program . . . In The Solution Of Student Housing Problems . . . We Want A Genuine Voice In Student Affairs NOW!

In spite of such signs of restiveness among the traditionally quiescent and apathetic student body, there is not much chance at present that the Brockport student body will take over the president's office, as the students at Columbia did the very day I visited Brockport. Given a much larger influx of black students and perhaps a few more white radicals, the odds would change.

One major problem at Brockport stems from the fact that half of the 1,800 incoming students are transfers, generally from junior colleges. Quite clearly this transfer business will increase, and this leads to the problems of articulation with the neighboring junior colleges. A question which elicits vigorous discussion on campuses like Brockport is whether, because of the growing numbers of transfers, the institution should phase out its first two years and become an upper-division and graduate institution. However, there is no thought of that at this time.

Brockport provides a program in the liberal arts during the first two years and then a variety of specialized academic major and minor programs during the last two years. All sorts of special new programs are being developed. Efforts are being made to set up relationships between the college and the urban ghetto in Rochester. For example, a group of Negro students is bussed out to the college's laboratory school for classes, and a large group of practice teachers spends an entire year living and teaching in Rochester, with the professors coming to them for their course work. An exchange program with the District of Columbia Teachers College is also in operation.

An interesting departure in curriculum is a special Peace Corps program, which enrolls students from the entire country in a 15-month program at the college, culminating in an A.B. degree and a teaching certificate plus Peace Corps training for work in the Dominican Republic. Students are given some credit toward graduate work, with the hope that after their two-year stint they will return to Brockport to complete the master's degree. One of the great concerns of the faculty is to diversify the student body in order to shake up the values of the generally homogeneous student body. The Peace Corps program brings to the campus some 60 students who are likely to do just this.

There is some use of educational television on the campus, and the computer center is growing in use as well. Biology and psychology have done some work toward setting up individualized programmed instruction in a few courses. There are plans afoot for training junior college teachers—a master's degree plus some kind of internship. The fine arts program is a source of pride to the faculty—as was the International Philosophic Year.

One could raise a question about the model Brockport has chosen for itself, for the thrust seems to be more toward a traditional liberal arts college than toward a multipurpose college. Indeed, Samuel Gould, chancellor of the state system, is reported to have referred to Amherst and Swarthmore as models for the state colleges. The name *College of Arts and Sciences* carries this connotation. What this means at Brockport, for example, is that there is an economics but no business major, which, I assume, would attract large numbers of local students. There seems to be relatively less talk about servicing the needs of Monroe County than about intellectual excellence and higher standards. Perhaps this is the way the place has to move at first. I hasten to add that some faculty members have exactly the contrary worry, namely, that Brockport will become too much of a service institution and forget about developing an intellectual base. Many plans for all sorts of community-related service and research programs, especially related to Rochester, are at the developmental stage.

What Brockport will be like in 1975 raises much speculation.

Some predict that the current 5,500 undergraduate enrollment will be 13,000 by then and that the figure for the graduate level will be 7,500. And with this growth in numbers, some predict, will come rapid expansion of both applied and professional schools as well as university status. Not only do some faculty predict that this will happen; many are gambling on it.

WESTERN MICHIGAN UNIVERSITY, KALAMAZOO A change in name does not necessarily mean a change in function. Many of the so-called state colleges are still very much single-purpose, teacher training institutions. Brockport is an example of a place where a name change has indeed meant a new institution. In like manner, one has to be wary of a name change from *state college* to *state university*. A place like the University of Northern Iowa is not really much further along than some institutions that are still called state colleges. However, Western Michigan University does seem to be well on its way toward becoming a fully developed regional university. If Kansas State Teachers College at Emporia illustrates an essentially single-purpose institution at one end of the spectrum and State University College at Brockport a developing institution somewhere along the middle of the spectrum, Western Michigan University, as a large multipurpose university, completes the spectrum.

Western Michigan University, serving southwestern Michigan, is located in Kalamazoo, a city of 100,000 people, located midway between Detroit and Chicago. It is a prosperous and progressive city with lots of industry as well as education. In addition to Western Michigan, there are Kalamazoo College, a small but enterprising and interesting liberal arts college; Nazareth College, a Catholic girls school; and Kalamazoo Valley Community College, which opened in the fall of 1968 with 850 full-time students and another 700 part-time students. There are a number of diversified industries in and around Kalamazoo, and many of these industries are well served by the large number of technological programs at Western Michigan.

Founded in 1903 as a normal school, Western has been through the usual changes. It was Western State Normal School, 1903; Western State Teachers College, 1927; Western Michigan College of Education, 1941; Western Michigan College, 1955; and finally Western Michigan University, 1957. Total enrollment stands at over 18,500 students. There are 900 faculty members. Among Michigan's institutions of higher education, Western Michigan ranks fourth—behind the University of Michigan, Michigan State University, and Wayne State University—in number of students, diversity and complexity, and level of academic programs. The first bachelor's degrees were authorized in 1918, and in December of 1968 the first doctoral degrees were conferred.

Growth is evident everywhere—a 50 percent increase in enrollment in five years, new dormitories and academic buildings. The large, expansive campus with its rolling terrain is really quite handsome and is dotted with new red-brick (called cranbrook brick) buildings and recently planted lawns and trees. A tour of the campus is bound to include the new $5 million complex: a 350-seat auditorium with its adjacent 600-seat university theater and liberal arts classroom building. An $8 million physical science building housing a 12-million-volt linear accelerator is under way, and recently opened is an impressive industrial and engineering technology building.

Teacher education remains central to the mission of the institution. About 60 percent of the undergraduates prepare to teach, a figure which has not changed much in recent years. Western Michigan ranks second in the United States in the number of teachers certified annually and first in the nation in the number of graduating students who enter the teaching profession. A number of interesting innovations are under way in teacher education, including an education specialist degree for the preparation of junior college teachers. This is a sixth-year program that enrolls, for the most part, people who already have their master's degrees. The motivation for these students is higher salary and a possible stepping stone toward the doctorate. The market for these people is great. There are about 25 junior colleges in Michigan now, with more to come. The program itself includes considerable work in an academic major plus cognate courses and six hours of professional education. The academic departments and the education people share responsibility for the program. At present, some 14 departments are involved.

Another innovation with great promise is the Center for Educational Studies jointly financed and run by Western Michigan and the Grand Rapids public schools. Too often, school systems and universities have operated in splendid isolation, each somewhat suspicious of the other. The center is a permanent part of both institutions and draws personnel from both places to conduct research, to disseminate research results, and to train schoolteachers as well as university students. Interdisciplinary in nature, the programs of the center involve faculty participation from political science, sociology, philosophy, and art, as well as education. Grand Rapids, 45 miles from Kalamazoo, is the second largest city in Michigan (population 300,000) and provides a large and complex but not unwieldy laboratory for research and study.

A Focus On Lateral Development

What really sets Western Michigan apart from Emporia and Brockport, aside from sheer size, is the breadth and complexity of its many applied programs. It is a multiversity. A vast array of undergraduate majors is at the base of 62 master's and 16 specialist degree programs. There is an Ed.D. degree offered, and Ph.D. programs have been introduced in chemistry (accredited by the American Chemical Society), mathematics, science education, and sociology. Physics is a possibility, but movement toward more doctoral work is not rapid. What especially impressed me is not this vertical movement, but rather the lateral movement into a number of areas which seem to have particular relevance to regional and state needs. Indeed, the degree of lateral movement at the undergraduate level in institutions of this kind is a better criterion of development than programs offered at the Ph.D. level.

The School of Applied Arts and Sciences is one of seven schools into which the university is divided. The others are Business, Education, Social Work, General Studies (which has basic responsibility for the general education program for all students), Liberal Arts and Sciences, and Graduate Studies. There is as well an Institute of International and Area Studies. When one adds all these to the many programs in the School of Applied Arts and Sciences, the result is an impressive variety aimed at professional and occupational goals.

Within the School of Applied Arts and Sciences are programs in agriculture, distributive education, engineering and technology, home economics, industrial education, military science, occupational therapy, paper technology, and transportation technology. The paper industry is big business in Michigan, and the undergraduate paper technology program is reputed to be superb and is known throughout the industry for its high standards. Industry, foundations, and individuals funnel money into the program in recognition of its importance to regional needs. The applied engineering programs are different from the more theoretical and abstract engineering science approaches fostered elsewhere at leading engineering institutions. The programs in civil, mechanical, metallurgical, electrical, and industrial engineering are designed to produce workaday, nuts-and-bolts technologists. The demand for this kind of person is very high. I am told the Detroit auto makers will hire all the graduates they can get from the automotive technology program. The same kind of program exists in aviation. In the School of Education, the graduate program in rehabilitation of the blind is well known, as is Western's department of speech pathology and audiology, which is one of only seven in the United States. The occupational therapy department is the largest in the nation. President James Miller at Western sees its job as educating the professional and subprofessional workers in the state, whether in the paper industry, in the classroom, or in other applied areas.

In meeting with a group of faculty members, most of them members of the executive committee of the faculty senate, I noted that all were from arts and sciences. Despite the prominence of the applied program, an excess of 50 percent of the faculty are in arts and sciences. Even so, this group seemed quite candid in saying there was not the usual infighting between arts and sciences and the applied areas that one generally finds elsewhere. I had heard that the morale at Western was high, and on my quick visit I found this to be the case. The faculty members with whom I spoke certainly feel that their institution is a university, though they do not seem overly anxious to develop doctoral programs ahead of what they regard as necessary resources in faculty and facilities.

Generally, they do not think there is too much emphasis upon research, though they do admit there is a problem in finding people willing to teach general education courses at the lower-division level. There was agreement that much of the so-called research that goes on at places like Western is "mission-oriented" rather than "pure." When asked about the willingness of the faculty to go along with the emphasis upon applied programs designed to meet the needs of the region, the general response was a favorable one, that it would be foolish for Western to use the University of Michigan as a model for itself. One faculty member even said that there was no real split between national and regional concerns. As he put it, "Through my discipline I have maintained identity with the national scene, but through my affiliation with the university I still feel very much a part of the region."

Perhaps there is a negative relationship between university status and the ability to attract faculty members interested in teaching lower-division students. Or, put another way, as one moves along the spectrum from single-purpose institutions toward multipurpose universities, concern about undergraduate teaching is reduced. Scholarly reputation with colleagues, research, and the like become overriding in importance, especially in matters of promotion and tenure.

It strikes me that Western Michigan is beginning to face the very kinds of problems that plague the older and more established universities and that have led some observers to wonder whether these institutions might do well to cut back drastically or to eliminate entirely their lower-division enrollments. When one looks at the actual flow of students through a place like Western Michigan, the question becomes much more than academic. The fact is that probably no more than about 50 percent of the graduates begin as freshmen at Western; there is a large exodus during the first two years and then a large inflow of students from community colleges and private colleges. The current ratio between upper- and lower-division students is about 3 to 2. When one questions the viability of the lower division at older institutions, cries of outrage issue forth; but at Western Michigan, despite the many objections raised to this suggestion, there seemed to be an open-mindedness among the few people with whom I spoke about the possibility of turning the institution into an upper-division and graduate place. This may be an indication of the ambitions of the institution, or at least of some people in it—that is, to specialize and professionalize their departments at the expense of the general student. As at many of the places I visited, over half the faculty have been at Western only a few years—a fact that creates problems in maintaining institutional coherence and unity of purpose.

Student Concerns and Financial Worries

I met with an interesting group of students: the editor of the *Western Herald,* the campus newspaper; the chairman of the homecoming; the vice-president and treasurer of the student association, an articulate critic of the general apathy of the student body; a leader in the Black Action Movement; a New York City Olympic athlete brought to Western by an athletic scholarship. He is also secretary-treasurer of the Black Action Movement.

We discussed what the students were like, with the general conclusion that in recent years there has been much more diversity at Western than before: vocational types, intellectuals, bohemians, socialites, and athletes. There is a little of everything, but the general flavor of the campus, according to these students, who obviously are active, is one of apathy and lack of concern about important issues—the typical kind of student in teacher education I found elsewhere. Yet there is no doubt that there is unrest here also, at least among a minority, including a protest group with long hair whose members call themselves Students for Social Involvement. The Black Action Movement, with about 500 members, has also been very active. There is no concerted drive to overthrow the administration, and the students with whom I spoke say that President Miller has gone out of his way to bring students into the administrative counsels of the institution through membership in important committees. Above all else, the students characterized Western as a very friendly place, and this seems to be the general feeling, as I indicated, among the faculty as well.

Interestingly, Western operates on a trimester system and everyone is happy—administration, faculty, and students. The first trimester goes from the first of September through Christmas, the second through mid-April, and the third is split into two sessions of 7½ weeks each. A student's course load in each of these two short sessions is cut in half, with courses meeting twice as long. Continuous full-time attendance allows completing the bachelor's degree program in 2 years and 8 months, though very few students seem to do this. Instead, most of them attend just the two regular trimesters during the year and are therefore out of school by mid-April—a fact which pleases them because they can land much better summer jobs before the rush of other students from other colleges. Enrollment in the third trimester is roughly half as large, and the administrators are happy to see the students leaving by mid-April because this eliminates riot fever in the springtime! The faculty is particularly content with the arrangement because their salary schedule is based not on the usual 9 months, but rather on a 7½-month work load. By teaching the extra 7½ weeks in the spring session, they get an additional 22 percent, a nice bonus. They are not allowed to teach an entire year of three trimesters. The second session of the third trimester is used primarily for graduate work for in-service teachers.

Finances are a problem. Fees are $370 per year for Michigan residents and $900 per year for nonresidents. Recent state appropriations are slightly over $800 per student. The state support does not meet the need. Enrollments are higher at the upper division, where costs are also higher, and the special applied programs cost much more than the arts and science programs. But despite these higher costs, the state continues to give financial support that puts Western not only far below the amount recommended for the University of Michigan, Michigan State, and Wayne State but also below what is recommended for some of the other public institutions.

President Miller is a political scientist with a decidedly New England accent. It turns out he is from Massachusetts and went to Amherst. He taught for a while at Michigan State and then became state comptroller under Gov. G. Mennen Williams. As such, he is thoroughly familiar with what goes on at the state level in Michigan, and no doubt his choice as president of Western Michigan in 1961 had something to do with his knowledge of state educational politics.

The recent history of educational politics in Michigan is interesting. Until 1963, Northern, Central, Eastern, and Western State Colleges had been under the state board of education, which apparently did not exercise very much control or interest in these institutions except to parcel out some money each year. In 1963, the new Michigan constitution established separate boards of trustees for each of these institutions, effectively divorcing them from public school authorities in the state. Meanwhile, the University of Michigan, having lost the battle in Michigan State's fight for university status, in effect gave up its struggle and did not contest the effort to make universities out of the state colleges in the late 1950s. Indeed, from the university's point of view, it was perhaps better to dilute Michigan State's power by calling all the state institutions *universities.* In any case, achieving university status for the state colleges was really no problem at all, including changing the College of Mining and Technology to Michigan Technology University. It is likely that Grand Valley College, Saginaw State College, and Ferris State College will soon go the university route as well.

Apparently, John Hannah, then president of Michigan State, and Harlan Hatcher, then president of the University of Michigan, did not want any kind of a state superboard for higher education for fear that such a board might take away the prestige and influence of their institutions. Consequently, the new constitution resulted in a dog-eat-dog struggle among the public institutions for budgetary support from the legislature. In theory, the state board of education coordinates and plans all education within the state and then advises the legislature and the governor. But in reality, the state board has no power and lacks the staff to accomplish much. The result is that budgets go directly to both the bureau of the budget and the state board. This, in turn, means that each president curries favor with the legislature. Michigan, Michigan State, and Wayne State have the largest constituencies, and a place like Western Michigan is at a disadvantage. Michigan State, in particular, with all its extension work is in the driver's seat. The fact that now some 35 percent of the students at Western Michigan come from the southeastern section, a more populous area of the state, may mean greater legislative support. This very brief recital of some of the political factors is illustrative of problems found in state after state across the nation where these emerging institutions must fight with the older established universities for their share of the public largess.

I might note that Western Michigan is on the nonmember list of the American Association of State Colleges and Universities (AASCU); that is, it is on the mailing list but does not pay dues. Though it may be misleading to attach any importance to this fact, voluntary organizational membership probably serves as a good indication of institutional self-image. I have the distinct impression that Western Michigan sees itself as a step removed from most of the membership of AASCU—and indeed it may be.

2. Some History and Numbers

In Peru, Nebraska, sits a small state college whose enrollment about matches the size of the community. An apocryphal story has it that after the Civil War a local state legislator lobbied hard on behalf of his constituency to have the state university located in Peru. This would have been a great honor and would have lent considerable prestige to the local boosters. He lost his battle but soon was pressing again, this time for location of the state prison at Peru. Again he lost out, but by then his legislative colleagues felt somewhat remiss and said that they would give Peru one of the new normal schools. "I don't know what it is, but we'll take it!" was his reply.

Not many people today know what it is either, for normal schools are historic relics. Lewis-Clark Normal School in Lewiston, Idaho, does exist, but the name may well be changed as the institution moves from a two-year program to a four-year program for both teachers and nonteachers. In Wisconsin, two-year county colleges for the preparation of elementary school teachers still remain as vestiges of the normal school movement. And there are many older women, some still teaching in elementary schools, who remember with warm nostalgia their experience at "The Normal" early in the century. A charming elderly woman, Mrs. Ruth Cormana of Harrington, Washington, described to me her education at the State Normal School at Cheney (now Eastern Washington State College) prior to World War I. Just retired after teaching since 1912, she feels her training served her well over the years.

The word *normal* means rule, model, or pattern. The job of the normal schools was to give prospective teachers models and rules for teaching. In 1910, there were 264 normal schools, enrolling 132,000 students. Of these 264 schools, 151 were run by the states, 40 by city and county authorities, and 73 by private sponsors.

They had their beginnings largely as a result of the missionary zeal of men like Horace Mann, who in the 1830s and 1840s successfully argued for common, or elementary, schools for all children. The phenomenal growth of elementary schools led inevitably to the question of teachers for these schools. James G. Carter in Massachusetts led the way toward the creation of public normal schools, in the tradition of European seminaries, to prepare teachers for this greatly expanded educational enterprise. The colonial colleges, largely enrolling men, simply did not provide enough elementary school teachers.

The case of New York was typical. Considerable debate took

TABLE 1 *State colleges and universities by decade and type of origin*

Decade	Academy or seminar	Normal or teachers college	Junior college	Multi-purpose state college	Technical, agricultural, etc.	Religious or YMCA	Total
Prior to 1800	1			1			2
1800-1809							
1810-1819	2						2
1820-1829	1						1
1830-1839	3	2			1	1	7
1840-1849	3	2		1			6
1850-1859	3	15					18
1860-1869		20			1	1	22
1870-1879	1	17			4	1	23
1880-1889	3	20			3	1	27
1890-1899	1	31		1	10	1	44
1900-1909		27			14	3	44
1910-1919		20	2		2		24
1920-1929		12	8	2			22
1930-1939			7	1	1		9
1940-1949			3	4	1		8
1950-1959			1	7	1		9
1960				11			11
TOTAL	18	166	21	28	38	8	279
Percent	6	59	8	10	14	3	100

SOURCE: Compiled by Carnegie Commission on Higher Education.

place in the 1830s and 1840s over the means for providing teachers for the schools. There was agreement about the need for teachers but disagreement about who should train them—the existing private academies or a new system of publicly financed state normal schools. The normal school idea smacked of Prussianism and strong central government. In addition, the private academies, which as secondary schools were forerunners to public high schools, already were preparing teachers for the elementary schools; and spread around the state geographically, they took the financial pinch off prospective teachers by providing them short, inexpensive courses. Important also was the fact that many people simply were not convinced that special professional training was either desirable or necessary. Whether education was an art or a science was debated then as now. In 1834, New York State provided funds to the private academies to subsidize their teacher training departments. Meanwhile, Carter was successful with his movements for public normal schools in Massachusetts. The first public normal school in the United States opened at Lexington, Massachusetts, in 1839. (Today this is the State College at Framingham.) The debate continued in New York, and finally, in 1844, the New York State Normal School at Albany came into existence.

Note that this was a school, not a college. The idea was to enroll elementary school graduates and to give them some professional work in pedagogy and then return them as teachers to the elementary schools about the state. Yet the students were so lacking in fundamental background that much of the work of the normal school was a thorough grounding in the common school subjects themselves—reading, writing, spelling, arithmetic, and geography. A regent's report in 1846 says, "Many had studied philosophy, whose spelling was deficient; and others studied algebra, who found it very difficult to explain intelligently the mystery of 'borrowing ten and carrying one' in simple subtraction." In addition, students were required to take vocal music, drawing, and English composition. Music and drawing, though not taught in the district schools, were supposed to sharpen the "faculties." Students were taught the methodology for teaching the common subjects as well as something about child development and the art of school government. The principal of the school was David Page, well known in the history of American education for his famous "normal chart of the elementary sounds of the English language," an early phonetic approach to the teaching of reading. The course was such that all the work in subject matter and pedagogy, including practice

TABLE 2
Total 1967
opening fall
enrollment
and number of
state colleges
and universities
by size and
census region

1967 total enrollment	New England	Middle Atlantic	East North Central	West North Central
Less than 1,000	3,616			2,815
(Number of institutions)	(8)			(4)
1,000-5,000	40,490	68,334	21,957	45,430
(Number of institutions)	(16)	(19)	(7)	(17)
5,000-10,000	36,894	94,772	93,405	54,144
(Number of institutions)	(5)	(13)	(13)	(8)
Over 10,000		20,805	160,018	34,052
(Number of institutions)		(1)	(11)	(3)
TOTAL	81,000	183,911	275,380	136,441
(Number of institutions)	(29)	(33)	(31)	(32)
Total U.S.	453,062	1,777,693	1,294,660	588,600
Percent of total U.S.	18	16	21	23
Total U.S. public control, 4-year	153,917	401,889	730,441	368,175
Percent	53	46	38	37

SOURCE: Compiled by Carnegie Commission on Higher Education from National Center for Educational Statistics, *Opening Fall Enrollment in Higher Education 1967,* U.S. Government Printing Office, 1967.

TABLE 3 *1967 opening fall enrollment of resident undergraduate and postbaccalaureate students in state colleges and universities by size and sex*

Size of institution	Total	Undergraduate					
		Full-time			Part-time		
		Men	Women	Total	Men	Women	Tota
Under 1,000 total	14,955	6,642	6,255	12,897	544	810	1,354
Percent	100	44	42	86	4	5	9
1,000-5,000 total	382,326	158,954	163,608	322,562	14,651	16,929	31,580
Percent	100	42	43	84	4	4	8
5,000-10,000 total	564,396	234,683	193,867	428,550	39,927	35,687	75,614
Percent	100	42	34	76	7	6	13
Over 10,000 total	418,648	155,131	124,603	279,734	36,717	30,958	67,675
Percent	100	37	30	67	9	7	16
TOTAL	1,380,325	555,410	488,333	1,043,743	91,839	84,384	176,223
Percent	100	40	35	76	7	6	13
Total U.S.	6,670,416	2,584,952	1,791,603	4,376,555	791,384	602,512	1,393,890
Percent	100	39	27	66	12	9	21
Percent of total U.S.	21	21	27	24	12	14	13

NOTE: Not all percents add to total percents because of rounding.

SOURCE: Compiled by Carnegie Commission on Higher Education from National Center for Educational Statistics, *Opening Fall Enrollment in Higher Education 1967, Supplement A, Undergraduate and Postbaccalaureate Students,* U.S. Government Printing Office, 1968.

South Atlantic	East South Central	West South Central	Mountain	Pacific	Outlying areas	Total
5,129			1,832	1,964		15,356
(7)			(2)	(3)		(24)
78,743	36,465	59,886	28,192	17,323	2,930	399,750
(33)	(13)	(20)	(11)	(6)	(2)	(144)
54,476	52,549	110,488	37,950	68,512		603,190
(7)	(7)	(15)	(5)	(9)		(82)
32,307	26,453	15,098		161,862		450,595
(3)	(2)	(1)		(8)		(29)
170,655	115,467	185,472	67,974	249,661	2,930	1,468,891
(50)	(22)	(36)	(18)	(26)	(2)	(279)
831,120	356,085	601,509	351,530	1,242,910	66,518	6,963,687
21	32	31	19	20	4	21
419,169	232,611	395,257	245,958	481,979	46,264	3,475,660
41	50	47	28	52	6	42

Postbaccalaureate					
Full-time			*Part-time*		
Men	Women	Total	Men	Women	Total
91	109	200	213	291	504
1	1	2	1	2	3
2,197	2,384	4,581	11,452	12,456	23,908
1	1	1	3	3	6
7,127	3,955	11,082	25,711	23,107	48,818
1	1	2	5	4	9
11,982	5,846	17,828	31,368	22,043	53,411
3	1	4	8	5	13
21,397	12,294	33,691	68,744	57,897	126,641
2	1	2	5	4	9
356,036	94,400	450,436	277,071	172,458	449,529
5	1	7	4	3	7
6	13	7	25	34	28

teaching, could be accomplished in one year. The summer term began in May; the winter term started in November and ended in April.

In the ensuing years, new educational ideas took hold in Albany and spread to other normal schools in New York. Pestalozzianism found root, as did Froebel's kindergarten. The school changed sites quite often, having commenced on the second floor of a railroad depot in Albany.

The future direction of Albany as well as of other normal schools was influenced directly by the rapid development of the high school movement. In New York, high schools could hire college graduates without pedagogical training or normal school graduates without subject-matter background. The normal schools did make some early attempts to provide teachers for secondary schools, placing "collegiate and scientific departments" alongside their one- and two-year normal school departments. Brockport, for example, included advanced English and classical courses of three and four

	Number of institutions		Total enrollment	
Size of institution	Number	Percent	Number	Percent
Less than 1,000 total enrollment	24	9	15,356 (100%)	1
1,000 - 5,000 total enrollment	144	52	399,750 (100%)	27
5,000 - 10,000 total enrollment	82	29	603,190 (100%)	41
Over 10,000 total enrollment	29	10	450,595 (100%)	31
TOTAL	279	100	1,468,891 (100%)	100
Total U.S.			6,963,687 (100%)	21
Total U.S. public 4-year institutions			3,475,660 (100%)	42

TABLE 4 *Total 1967 opening fall enrollment in state colleges and universities by size and sex*

SOURCE: Compiled by Carnegie Commission on Higher Education from National Center for Educational Statistics, *Opening Fall Enrollment in Higher Education 1967*, U.S. Government Printing Office, 1967.

years at the same time that their elementary teachers were graduated in two years.

Matters came to a head in the 1880s as more and more teachers
were needed for the growing high school population. Growth of the
public high schools after the Civil War was clearly the most important factor in bringing about the transformation of the normal
schools into teachers colleges throughout the United States. The
teachers had to keep at least one step ahead of their students. There
were other factors, including the growth of teacher training in public state universities, the expansion of what constituted professional
education, and growing pressures for higher standards from incip-
ient accrediting agencies. In any case, the Normal School at Albany
became New York Normal College in 1890, requiring high school
graduation for entrance. Interestingly, the *entire* instruction was
restricted to professional education: methods, school management,
philosophy, and history of education. The assumption was that by
requiring high school graduation for admission, students knew

Men		Women	
Number	Percent	Number	Percent
7,669	1	7,687	1
(50%)		(50%)	
196,675	25	203,075	30
(49%)		(51%)	
325,243	42	277,947	40
(54%)		(46%)	
248,660	32	201,935	29
(55%)		(45%)	
778,247	100	690,644	100
(53%)		(47%)	
4,158,557	19	2,805,130	25
(60%)		(40%)	
2,022,665	38	1,452,995	48
(58%)		(42%)	

enough subject matter to teach at the high school level. All they needed was a good dose of professional education. An appeal was made also to college graduates to take a short course in pedagogy to prepare as teachers—a forerunner of the modern master of arts in teaching programs.

Gradually the conclusion was reached that teachers ought to have some additional academic as well as pedagogical training. In 1914, New York State Normal College became New York State College for Teachers. This change was considered highly significant, and even today the point is strongly made that since 1914 the emphasis at Albany has been upon the word *college* and not upon *teachers.* In short, this was to be basically a liberal arts college preparing people for work in the secondary schools, the elementary program having been dropped in 1906. The A.B. degree was soon introduced, and this meant that by 1948, when the State University of New York was established, there had been a fairly long tradition of undergraduate majors and academic disciplines at Albany. This was in sharp contrast to the other public colleges in New York. It meant that students from all over the state came to Albany.

This former normal school preparing young women for elemen-

		Full-time		Part-time	
Size of institution	*Total enrollment*	*Number*	*Percent*	*Number*	*Percent*
Less than 1,000 *total enrollment*	15,356 (100%)	13,097 (85%)	1	1,858 (12%)	1
1,000 - 5,000 *total enrollment*	399,750 (100%)	327,143 (82%)	30	54,430 (14%)	18
5,000 - 10,000 *total enrollment*	603,190 (100%)	440,582 (73%)	41	124,952 (21%)	41
Over 10,000 *total enrollment*	450,595 (100%)	297,647 (66%)	28	121,285 (27%)	40
TOTAL	1,468,981 (100%)	1,078,469 (73%)	100	302,525 (21%)	100
Total U.S.	6,963,687 (100%)	4,826,991 (69%)	22	1,843,425 (26%)	16
Total U.S. public *4-year institutions*	3,475,660 (100%)	2,575,706 (74%)	42	679,199 (20%)	45

TABLE 5 *Full-time, part-time, extension, and first-time freshmen 1967 opening fall enrollment in state colleges and universities by size of institution*

*Less than 1 percent.

SOURCE: Compiled by Carnegie Commission on Higher Education from National Center for Educational Statistics, *Opening Fall Enrollment in Higher Education 1967,* U.S. Government Printing Office, 1967.

tary teaching is now one of the four major university centers within the SUNY system. It has been building since 1962 toward comprehensive university status. The Ph.D., now given in 19 areas, will be given in all the arts and sciences; advanced degrees are given in education, business, library, social work, nursing, and criminal justice. With the most striking architecture to be found on any college campus in the country, Albany has come a long way since its days on the second floor of the railroad depot. Like the University of California at Los Angeles, Albany has come the full route from normal school to university. Just as UCLA is not a member of AASCU, so one might expect Albany soon to disassociate itself from this group of institutions.

Few of the AASCU member institutions began as early as Albany or have changed as much. All have different histories, yet most of the 279 institutions were normal schools or teachers colleges at some point. In fact, 166 (59 percent) began that way. Another 38 (14 percent) started life as agricultural or technical institutes, 28 (10 percent) as state colleges, 21 (8 percent) as junior colleges, 18 (6 percent) as academies or seminaries, and 8 (3 percent) as religious schools or YMCAs.

Their origins seem to group chronologically into four distinct

Extension		First-time freshmen	
Number	Percent	Number	Percent
401 (3%)	*	4,446 (29%)	1
18,177 (4%)	21	98,949 (25%)	33
37,656 (6%)	43	129,720 (22%)	43
31.663 (7%)	36	70,270 (16%)	23
87,897 (6%)	100	303,385 (21%)	100
293,271 (5%)	30	1,652,317 (24%)	18
220,755 (6%)	40	650,875 (19%)	47

periods (Table 1). The period before 1850 was the age of the academy, and 10 of the 18 academies were started in that era. The period 1850-1920 belonged to the normal school and, later in the period, to the teachers college; no less than 150 were founded, 58 of them between 1890 and 1910. The remaining institutions, begun between 1850 and 1920, were almost all technical and agricultural institutes, and most of these likewise were founded between 1890 and 1910.

The third period belongs to the junior college and covers 1920 to 1940. Fifteen of the 21 current state colleges and universities that began as junior colleges were founded in this period. In all, 31 AASCU institutions were founded between 1920 and 1940. The fourth period, 1940 to the present, is characterized by the establishment of comprehensive state colleges. Twenty-two of the 28 AASCU institutions that were founded in this period originated as state colleges.

Though the individual institutional histories obviously differ, a general historical pattern is clear. If the institution is very old, it is likely that it was founded as an academy or seminary and then evolved into a normal school during the period when most of the other normal schools were being founded — usually prior to the turn of the century. The religious schools and those under the auspices of the YMCA also became normal schools when they came under

TABLE 6
Total number of teachers eligible for initial certification in state colleges and universities by size of institution, 1965-66

1967 size of institution	Teachers eligible for initial certification
Less than 1,000 total enrollment (10 institutions reporting)	1,075
1,000-5,000 total enrollment (121 institutions reporting)	28,589
5,000-10,000 total enrollment (75 institutions reporting)	33,076
Over 10,000 total enrollment (27 institutions reporting)	21,551
TOTAL (233 institutions reporting)	84,291
Total U.S. (901 institutions reporting)	181,048
Percent of total U.S.	47

SOURCE: Compiled by Carnegie Commission on Higher Education from The American Association of Colleges for Teacher Education, *Teacher Productivity— 1966,* Washington, D.C., 1967.

state control, principally because of financial pressure. A few of the agricultural and technical institutes, mostly those founded for Negroes, likewise became normal schools, but most expanded their offerings and skipped over the normal school phase. In the same way, the more recently founded junior colleges became state colleges without going through the normal school phase at about the time the normal schools and teachers colleges were becoming state colleges and expanding their curriculum. Today new state colleges are being founded at the time that many existing state colleges are becoming universities.

In sum, there seems to be an evolution in the present AASCU membership. The normal school to prepare elementary teachers becomes a teachers college to prepare secondary as well as elementary teachers. Then as the state seeks to respond to increasing demands for higher education, the teachers college expands its function and enlarges its enrollment and curriculum to become a multipurpose state college and perhaps a university.

AASCU MEMBERS: ENROLLMENTS AND TEACHERS PRODUCED These 279 institutions are spread widely around the country (Table 2). Fifty of them are found in the South Atlantic area, far more than the average of about thirty found in other sections of the country. The Mountain states are low, with 18. Though leader in the number of institutions, the South Atlantic region lags behind in total enrollment because the colleges are not large. The North Central area leads in number of students.

Nationwide in 1967, there were 1.47 million students enrolled, or 21 percent of all students in higher education. And this figure is fairly consistent across the country, though low in New England and the Middle Atlantic areas. Nationwide, 42 percent of the students in public four-year institutions are in these state colleges and regional universities. Residential, full-time students comprise most of the enrollment (Table 3).

Twenty-four of the 279 institutions have enrollments under 1,000 and account for only 1 percent of the enrollment in state colleges and universities (Table 4). Twenty-seven percent of the enrollment is found in the 144 colleges with 1,000 to 5,000 students. Eighty-two medium-large places with enrollments of 5,000 to 10,000 have 41 percent of the students. The 29 large institutions with enrollments over 10,000 have 31 percent of the students. These large places are found mostly on the West Coast and in the eastern part of the North Central region.

When we look at the distribution of men and women by size

of institution, an interesting fact emerges. Overall, these colleges enroll 53 percent men and 47 percent women, or just about the national average. Bearing in mind the heavy predominance of women in the early history of most of the state colleges, this change in the sex balance is a noteworthy development. It reflects the move from the preparation of elementary teachers to that of secondary teachers as well, the gradual development of liberal arts and applied programs as these colleges became multipurpose institutions, and in recent times, the heavy demand for and short supply of college spaces. Interestingly, the smaller the institution, the higher the percentage of women students, so that, for example, there are just as many women as men in the two smallest categories of institutions. These are, no doubt, mainly single-purpose, teacher training colleges, concentrating on elementary education.

The figures for the state colleges and regional universities parallel those for all higher education when it comes to part-time and extension students (Table 5). Seventy-three percent are full-time students, 21 percent are part-time, and 6 percent are extension students. But again, the size of the institution makes a difference. Eighty-five percent of the students at the smallest institutions are full-time, whereas only 66 percent at the largest places are full-time students. In like manner, first-time freshman enrollments are considerably higher at the smaller institutions than at the large ones, where incoming transfer students from other colleges help to swell upper-division classes. Twenty-nine percent of the stu-

TABLE 7 Earned degrees conferred 1965-66 at state colleges and universities by size of institution and level of degree	Bachelor's	
1967 total enrollment	*Number of degrees*	*Number of institution conferring*
Under 1,000	1,768	17
1,000-5,000	38,566	130
5,000-10,000	52,487	80
Over 10,000	42,412	29
TOTAL	135,233	266
Total U.S.	524,117	
Percent of total U.S.	26%	

SOURCE: Compiled by Carnegie Commission on Higher Education from National Center for Educational Statistics, *Earned Degrees Conferred, 1965-66,* U.S. Government Printing Office, 1965.

dents at the smallest places are first-time freshmen; the corresponding figure is 16 percent at the largest places.

Many people are unaware that teacher education is big business in *all* higher education, not just in the former teachers colleges. Eight of the first ten leading producers of teachers in the United States are major state universities, not state colleges or regional universities. Michigan State was number one in 1967. Indeed, one-third of all bachelor's degrees in the United States go to people prepared as teachers. But teacher education is even bigger business in state colleges (Table 6). About 47 percent of America's teachers are prepared at state colleges, and these represent about 62 percent of those receiving baccalaureate degrees from these institutions: 61 percent of the graduates of the smallest institutions are prepared to teach, 74 percent from the 1,000 to 5,000 category, 63 percent from the 5,000 to 10,000 category, and 51 percent from the largest places. State colleges and regional universities grant 26 percent of all bachelor's degrees, 18 percent of all master's degrees, and 1 percent of doctorates and so-called first professional degrees (Table 7).

Another Carnegie Commission Profile is aimed specifically at the problems of predominantly Negro colleges, both public and private. Consequently, this study will not attempt to describe their very special sets of problems. But it should be noted that among the 279 state colleges and regional universities, 18 are predominantly Negro institutions, found, for the most part, in the

First professional		Master's		Doctor's	
Number of degrees	Number of institutions conferring	Number of degrees	Number of institutions conferring	Number of degrees	Number of institutions conferring
		14	1		
10	2	5,230	78	12	1
103	2	10,283	73	78	7
311	4	10,283	28	178	10
424	8	25,810	180	268	18
31,496		140,772		18,239	
1%		18%	1%		

TABLE 8				
	1967 total enrollment	Number of institutions reporting	Total	White
Less than 1,000		14	10,069 (100%)	7,003 (70%)
	(Negro colleges)	(4)	(2,564)	(99)
	(Percent of total)	(29)	(25)	(1)
1,000-5,000		141	346,514 (100%)	302,433 (87%)
	(Negro colleges)	(14)	(32,316)	(1,212)
	(Percent of total)	(10)	(9)	(*)
5,000-10,000		81	471,973 (100%)	455,434 (96%)
Over 10,000		29	337,240 (100%)	319,564 (95%)
	TOTAL	265	1,165,796 (100%)	1,084,434 (93%)
	(Negro colleges)	(18)	(34,880)	(1,311)
	(Percent of total)	(7)	(3)	(*)
	Total U.S. (in survey)		4,764,834 (100%)	4,393,768 (92%)

Table 8: Fall 1967 undergraduate enrollment by race in state colleges and universities (with over 500 undergraduates) by size of institution

*Less than 0.5 percent.

SOURCE: Compiled by Carnegie Commission on Higher Education from *The Chronicle of Higher Education,* vol. II, no. 16, pp. 3-4, April 22, 1968.

		Percent increase 1966-1975		
	Size of institution	Undergraduate	Graduate	Total
	Less than 1,000 total 1967 enrollment	+257	*	+271
	1,000-5,000 total 1967 enrollment	+96	+159	+101
	5,000-10,000 total 1967 enrollment	+94	+168	+102
	Over 10,000 total 1967 enrollment	+64	+96	+69
	TOTAL	+87	+134	+92

Table 9: Institutional estimates of percent increases in total enrollment to 1975 in state colleges and universities by size of institution and level of enrollment

*Over 1,000 percent.

SOURCE: Compiled by Carnegie Commission on Higher Education from questionnaires sent to institutions by American Association of State Colleges and Universities.

Negro	Other
2,956	110
(29%)	(1%)
(2,450)	(15)
(83)	(14)
36,224	7,857
(10%)	(3%)
30,982)	(122)
(86)	(2)
9,077	7,462
(2%)	(2%)
9,368	8,308
(3%)	(2%)
57,625	23,737
(5%)	(2%)
33,432)	(137)
(58)	(1)
45,410	125,656
(5%)	(3%)

verage annual percent increase 1966 - 1975		
ndergraduate	*Graduate*	*Total*
+15.2	+32.8	+15.7
+7.7	+11.1	+8.0
+7.6	+11.6	+8.2
+5.6	+7.7	+6.0
+7.2	+9.9	+7.5

South—Alabama State College, Jackson State College, and Grambling College are examples. Four of the Negro state colleges enroll fewer than 1,000 students, while the other 14 enroll as many as 5,000 students (Table 8).

The distribution of Negro students among all 279 institutions as a whole almost parallels national figures. That is, about 5 percent of the students in American higher education are Negroes, and about half of these are found in predominantly Negro colleges. Among the state colleges and regional universities, Negro enrollments are 5 percent of the total, but of this, 58 percent are found in Negro colleges. This means that in these state institutions, supposedly in business to meet the need for mass education, the percentage of Negroes, on the whole, is no higher, and indeed may be lower, than in many private institutions much more selective in their admissions procedures. In short, the state colleges have not as yet done much to expand Negro enrollments, though in several of the institutions I visited special recruitment drives and programs were under way.

I noted that 8 percent of the state colleges and universities began as junior colleges. I had expected this percentage to be much higher.

TABLE 10
Projected total enrollment in state colleges and universities

Size of institution	1966		
	Undergraduate	*Graduate*	*Tot*
Less than 1,000 total	6,779	102	6,88
1967 enrollment	99%	1%	10
(Number of institutions reporting)	(13)	(13)	(1
1,000-5,000 total 1967	261,195	22,244	283,43
enrollment	92%	8%	10
(Number of institutions reporting)	(112)	(112)	(11
5,000-10,000 total 1967	363,326	48,009	423,92
enrollment	88%	22%	10
(Number of institutions reporting)	(64)	(64)	(6
Over 10,000 total 1967	252,048	58,883	333,44
enrollment	81%	19%	10
(Number of institutions reporting)	(23)	(23)	(2
TOTAL	883,348	129,238	1,047,68
	87%	13%	10
(Number of institutions reporting)	(212)	(212)	(21

NOTE: Undergraduate and graduate figures do not add to total because not all schools gave breakdowns.

SOURCE: Compiled by Carnegie Commission on Higher Education from questionnaires sent to institutions by American Association of State Colleges and Universities.

Just as the progression from normal school to teachers college to state college to university means climbing the ladder of prestige and development, so one might think that similar pressures were great for two-year colleges to become four-year colleges. Between 1920 and 1940, 15 of the 21 made the change. Since that time, there have not been many community colleges that have taken on four-year state college status. Missouri Southern State College, in Joplin, is in the process of adding a diversified program at the upper-division level on top of the typical open-door community college lower-division program. But its change is the exception. One good reason for the lack of expansionist sentiment among community college people is the success of the junior college movement itself. It has now achieved momentum and status of its own, and there is no great need to mimic the state colleges.

Projected enrollments in state colleges and universities until 1975 show an overall 92 percent increase from 1966—87 percent at the undergraduate level and 134 percent at the graduate level (Tables 9 and 10). If institutional projections are correct, by 1975 all the institutions will have moved up one notch in the enrollment category. The typical institution will more than double in size, from

	1975	
dergraduate	*Graduate*	*Total*
24,226	1,316	25,542
95%	5%	100%
(13)	(13)	(13)
510,711	57,588	568,299
90%	10%	100%
(112)	(112)	(112)
703,575	128,795	855,732
85%	15%	100%
(64)	(64)	(66)
413,874	115,150	565,026
78%	22%	100%
(23)	(23)	(25)
552,386	302,849	2,014,599
85%	15%	100%
(212)	(212)	(216)

4,500 to 10,000. Leaving aside the creation of additional institutions, this would mean that by 1975 AASCU will have a constituency of institutions serving incredibly large and diverse student bodies. The smallest 24 institutions will average about 2,000 students. The next 144 will average over 5,000 in total enrollment. Eighty-two institutions will average about 13,000 students, and the current 29 which are the largest will be pushed into a new category, with an average of over 22,000. These averages, of course, do not tell the whole story, for even today the variation in size is extraordinary—from total enrollments over 20,000 at California State College at Los Angeles (21,350), San Diego State College (30,077), San Francisco State (25,585), and the State University of New York at Buffalo (20,600) down to the smallest institution at the present time, Massachusetts Maritime Academy with 205 students. I shall return to this issue of size.

It does not take long for one to sense the importance of status among different kinds of institutions. It is readily evident through the associations they choose to join. At the top in prestige, though not in political influence, is the Association of American Universities (AAU), a kind of clubby group of the major public and private research universities. The Association of American Colleges (AAC) is a large group of diverse institutions whose hallmark is that they are private. After some infighting, the state universities and land-grant colleges resolved some of their differences and merged into an organization with considerable political clout known as the National Association of State Universities and Land-Grant Colleges (NASULGC). Below that, a newcomer on the scene, is the American Association of State Colleges and Universities (AASCU), and below that is the American Association of Junior Colleges (AAJC). One of the ironies within this alphabet soup is that the junior college group is flexing its muscles like a young adolescent and is a cause for concern among its older four-year colleagues as a potent political force. The distinction between a state university which is a member of NASULGC and that which is a member of AASCU is the distinction in the minds of some between high prestige and statewide programs on the one hand and regionally oriented programs and lower prestige on the other. It is the difference, as I pointed out earlier, between a Michigan State University and University of Michigan on the one hand and a Central Michigan or Eastern Michigan University on the other hand.

There has been a close association between NASULGC and

AASCU. They have held their annual meetings together and often join on common policy statements. I raise a question whether this close assocation is a healthy one for AASCU members, who, I would argue, need to strike out on their own in new directions and seek their own identity apart from established and often conservative institutions. In fact, the junior colleges (AAJC) and the state colleges (AASCU) as developing institutions have more in common than do the state colleges and the NASULGC institutions. They share the problems of fantastic growth and the need for new solutions to the question of mass education. Their educational programs are inextricably linked as junior college transfers mount in numbers and as the state colleges become a major source of junior college teachers. In short, my own observation—heretical as it may be—is that AASCU would benefit from less association with NASULGC and more association with AAJC.

3. Educational Pressures: Internal and External

One obvious characteristic of these emerging state colleges is change—and this means problems. Rapid growth in itself produces all sorts of strain in the network of relationships involved in the running of a college or university. Then there is the complication of deciding just what the function of these state colleges and universities ought to be, the "identity crisis" of which Clark Kerr speaks.

These problems would be tough enough if each institution were to make its own decisions, but increasingly these days institutional decisions—whether at the faculty, administrative, or trustee level— must dovetail with the overall interests of the state as determined by boards of higher education, coordinating councils, and the like. In turn, these state agencies must make decisions bearing in mind the total financial resources of the state and the competing demands from every side. All these elements are entangled with one another, and it is difficult to pull them apart. But when one adds to the boiling pot of problems the traditions, folklore, and legalities of 50 individual states as well as the idiosyncratic behavior of thousands of individuals looking at higher education from particular points of view, one despairs of any form of reliable generalization. But patterns do emerge.

INTERNAL PRESSURE: FROM SOFTNESS TO HARDNESS David Riesman uses the image of softness and hardness to describe the changes that take place as former teachers colleges become general colleges and universities. As we have seen, the old normal schools in preparing elementary teachers enrolled mostly women. The warmth and friendliness one still feels at many of these institutions is undoubtedly related to a strong tradition of feminine influence. Moreover, the behavioral sciences in general, and education in particular, have been labeled *soft*, as opposed to hard sciences like physics and chemistry. This softness implies a lack of intellectual rigor, and indeed programs in education have been notorious in the past for just that. In addition, teachers colleges devoted to preparation of elementary teachers did not really have solid, or *hard*, majors but rather a succession of minors for the general-purpose teacher. Finally, as one might expect, there were heavy percentages of women on the faculties of the old teachers colleges.

As these institutions began to prepare more secondary teachers, the image of softness began to change. Upper-division majors had to be introduced, and this meant bringing in faculty members with Ph.D.'s in subject fields, rather than Ed.D. degrees (doctor of education). A new hardness appeared. More male faculty members appeared on the campus, and the sex balance of the student body changed significantly. This process accelerates rapidly as non-teaching programs are introduced, including the straight A.B. degree. Male students begin to outnumber the female students, the academic disciplines assert themselves at the upper-division and graduate levels, and hardness and impersonality develop within the campus culture. The older education faculty together with old guard academic people concerned about general education no longer control the votes within the faculty as the academic and applied departments expand their size and numbers. The new breed faculty call for higher standards in undergraduate admissions and are tougher in their grading. This new breed is far more concerned with inducting new professionals into the academic guild than with preparing warm and dedicated teachers for the public schools. General education courses are increasingly difficult to staff; faculty want to teach only upper-division and graduate courses. The new faculty show more concern for and knowledge about their disciplines and colleagues within that discipline at other institutions than about their own institution and colleagues in other departments on their own campus.

This metaphorical change from softness to hardness means the introduction of a great deal more competition. The students begin to compete with one another for grades; the faculty begin to compete with one another for promotion and tenure on the basis of publications and research; and the institution itself begins to compete strenuously for state and federal money for operating expenses, buildings, and research.

One noticeable and important exception to the change from

softness to hardness has to do with college administration. The presidents of the former teachers colleges were inevitably Ed.D.'s and not Ph.D.'s. They came from teacher education backgrounds themselves, often had been public school teachers and school super-intendents, and then possibly had been professors of education. Though the traditions within public education can be labeled *soft*, the tradition of educational administration can be labeled *hard*. That is, school administrators over the years have tended to be authoritarian and autocratic in the running of "their" schools. One never refers to an Ed.D. without calling him "Doctor"; his secre-tary is sure to make the correction if an error is made! This concern for status and authority carries right over to college administration. In those institutions where the presidents are Ed.D.'s one is likely to find a great deal more deference paid to the president in terms of title and protocol than, for example, at places like Harvard or Princeton.

In fact, one can almost make the generalization that the less pres-tigious the institution or the less fully developed, the more powerful the president. The Negro colleges have been notorious for their authoritarian presidents, and I would hazard the generalization that those state colleges which have moved the least along the spec-trum from single-purpose teacher training to multipurpose uni-versity likewise centralize a great deal of power and authority with-in the president's office.

This is due partly at least to the small size of many of the former teachers colleges. The total administrative staff usually numbered no more than half a dozen. The president with an academic dean and a few directors ran the institution, and the president was in-volved in just about every decision. Some change became inev-itable as the institution grew in size, but this very growth in many cases depended largely upon the direct influence of policies orig-inating with the president.

One often hears that the age of the hero is dead. This is certainly not true when it comes to the administration of state colleges and regional universities. There is just no doubt whatsoever that the reputations of these institutions are directly related to the leader-ship exercised by their presidents. Men like John Emens at Ball State and John W. Maucker at the University of Northern Iowa have almost literally put their institutions on the map. One of the major problems facing institutions of this kind is finding the ad-ministrative leadership necessary for greater development. There is an acute shortage of first-rate presidential candidates as well as able administrators down through the ranks.

Ironically, first-rate presidents often become the means of their own undoing. The enterprising president pushing his institution along the route toward university status has the recruitment of top-quality faculty with Ph.D.'s from respected graduate schools high on his agenda. This new faculty is not about to accept the traditional authority and prestige of the Ed.D. president. The first thing that happens is that noises are made about increased faculty participation in governance. The old faculty committees to which the president may have paid lip service when it came to major decisions simply are no longer acceptable. The new faculty wants greater participation in policy decisions; they want to exercise the same degree of faculty control found in the institutions from which they came. Again, bear in mind the generalization that the more prestigious the institution, the less the power of the president and the greater the power of the faculty. One result is the creation of faculty senates on state colleges and campuses all over the country.

Faculty senates build into the governance of the institution a faculty voice in policy decisions. One problem in many of these new faculty senates is that very often the senate members are unable to differentiate between policy making and administration—a common problem in areas other than education! But many hours are now spent deliberating over relatively minor matters that have more to do with the nuts and bolts of administration than with weighty policy issues.

But the point to be made is that a strong educationist president in developing his institution thereby begins to undercut his own authority. The final blow comes when the new breed faculty which he has recruited turns on him, in effect, by insisting that there must be an academic Ph.D., not an education Ed.D., as president! One way to place the movement of an institution across the spectrum of development and changing status is simply to learn something of the background of the president of the institution. With very few exceptions, those places that have moved the farthest have academic types as leaders. As an illustration, when the state college system in California came into being in 1960, the vast bulk of the state college presidents were in some way or other connected with public education. Now, of the nineteen presidents only two are from public education and a third has a degree in higher education. As a group, the California colleges are as far along the spectrum of development as any in the country.

To mention California is to bring to mind the influence of state systems and coordinating councils upon developments at individual campuses. At the very time that internal governance is an issue, the matter is complicated by the increasingly powerful role played by state agencies in external governance.

Looked to for several years as the model for a statewide system of higher education, California is now in deep trouble. The famous Master Plan for Higher Education in California 1960-1975 has been under severe attack. The pressures are many and diverse. The Legislative Joint Committee on Higher Education, chaired by Jesse Unruh, former speaker of the assembly, came up with a suggestion for a radical revision of the structure and governance of public higher education within the state. At the same time, the state colleges have about reached the point of explosion with respect to their status within the system. All this leaves aside the open warfare between Gov. Ronald Reagan and higher education.

The people of California accept higher education just as they do the sunshine. Tuition-free, open-door access to some form of first-rate college education is very much taken for granted by the public at large. The reputation of Berkeley is challenged only by that of Harvard as the top university in the nation, if not in the world. The other campuses of the University of California are distinguished in their own right. At the same time, the 85 or so local community colleges are the most fully developed in the country, and all the states that are Johnny-come-lately to the community college movement look to California for advice.

In the middle is the state college system, with 18 colleges now in operation and more to open. Prior to World War II, there were seven state colleges, with 13,000 students. Enrollments in the state colleges currently exceed 170,000 students and are expected to reach 225,000 by 1970 and 300,000 by 1980. Although the oldest of the colleges, San Jose, dates back to 1857, the California state college system under an independent board of trustees was created by the legislation implementing the master plan in 1960. Previously, as in many states where the primary function of these institutions was to prepare teachers, the colleges were under the jurisdiction of the state board of education.

The master plan established a layer-cake system of the university, state colleges, and junior colleges and also established the Coordinating Council for Higher Education. The functions of the state colleges were set forth as follows:

The primary function of the state colleges is the provision of instruction for undergraduate students and graduate students through the master's degree, in the liberal arts and sciences, in applied fields and in the professions, including the teaching profession. . . . The doctoral degree may be awarded jointly with the University of California. Faculty research is authorized to the extent that it is consistent with the primary function of the state colleges and facilities provided for that function.

The multicampus university was to be the center for research and was to enroll undergraduates from the top 12.5 percent of their high school graduating classes. The state colleges were clearly to continue their role in training teachers but were to include other applied areas as well and were to enroll students from the top third of their graduating classes. The community colleges, on the other hand, were to be open to all high school graduates and were to offer a variety of college-transfer and occupational-terminal programs.

The master plan very neatly differentiated the functions of the three elements in public higher education. One unintended result of differentiation of students by the usual academic criteria was differentiation by race and social class. Black and brown students found themselves, because of their school records, pretty much excluded from the university and the state colleges. Black enrollment at San Francisco State College, for example, actually declined from about 11 percent before the master plan to about 3 percent at the time of the strike in 1968. Despite adjustments in admissions requirements, the discontent of minority students has been a major reason for strife in many California state colleges.

Minority students feel like second-class citizens; many state college faculty members and administrators feel that way, too. Indeed, the problem child in the system has been the state colleges: they are not content with the functions assigned to them. This is not a phenomenon unique to California. "The universities have a good idea what their job is, and the community colleges have carved out a niche for themselves. Our problem is with the state colleges. They occupy a no-man's-land in the middle, with overlapping responsibilities for mass education with the community colleges and yet with ambitions for research and doctoral work that tread on the ground of the university." These comments come from an official in another large state with responsibility for coordinating public higher education.

Glenn Dumke, chancellor of the California state colleges, believes in differentiation of function but only if all the elements feel parity of status, which is precisely what the state colleges have not achieved. To this end, he outlined a five-point program in 1968 aimed at making the state colleges first-class citizens in California higher education. Among his points was salary parity with the University of California. The salaries are not now far apart except at the highest levels. Another point was change of name to the California State University. Dumke feels strongly that these institutions are in fact universities now, especially when one compares them with many of the private institutions which call themselves universities — California Western, Redlands, the University of the Pacific. These seem like small liberal arts colleges in comparison with a place like San Diego State, for example. Related to this recommendation was one for a reduction in faculty teaching loads from the present average of 12 hours per week to 9 hours in order to match the university faculty load. He called for an introduction of Ph.D. programs with an emphasis upon the preparation of college teachers. Finally, he asked for additional funds from the legislature to expand fringe benefits, including sabbatical leaves.

In turn, Dumke has been accused by the university people of attempting to break the master plan. At the same time, his office is under attack from his own state college people for many reasons, including the undifferentiated treatment of the state colleges, with their diverse needs and uneven rates of development. Some feel that it is a fatal error to insist on equal speed on every campus in "pursuit of the Holy Grail" of university status and doctoral programs. The result is said to be a generalized mediocrity imposed on all institutions by the chancellor's office. Administration is by formula rather than by analysis of particular need. The complaint is that the chancellor's office simply will not put money where the action is but has instead chosen to follow the politically expedient route of bringing everyone along together.

But the main issue with the state colleges is clear: second-class citizenship alongside the university. As one man metaphorically put it, "We haven't arrived yet, but someday we'll play in the Rose Bowl." Obvious issues are doctoral programs and university status. State college people see no reason why specific departments, when ready, should not undertake doctoral programs, especially in areas of the curriculum not covered by the university. As it is, joint doctoral programs exist between San Diego State College and Berkeley in chemistry and genetics, between San Francisco State and Berkeley in special education, and between Cal State at Los Angeles and UCLA also in special education. Many faculty members in the state colleges are irked by the implicit assumption that they are inadequate to the task of putting together quality doctoral programs. I did not find that faculty members were overly concerned about the name *university*, except insofar as the name *state college* hinders recruitment of faculty who would rather locate at a university.

The advantages of teaching in California are obvious: high pay, sunshine, and vacationland atmosphere. The result has been the success until very recently of national recruiting efforts to build strong state college faculties. The irony is that this success is an element in the bitterness that exists. These faculties insist on first-class seats; they do not want the tourist-cabin service. Though it is true that the pay is good, their salaries still lag behind university salaries. Fringe benefits, including sabbatical arrangements, are much better at the university. Whereas university professors have no problem arranging for payment of graduate assistants for research, money is unavailable for this purpose at the state colleges. The 12-hour teaching load at the state colleges is significantly higher than at the university. The strategy of the American Federation of Teachers in 1968 was to work on this particular problem.

There have been a total of five organizations vying for faculty allegiance. The AFT is the most militant and has about 1,000 members of the total 9,000 faculty in the California system. The AFT has tried to organize the entire system but has failed so far. Far less militant is the Association of State College Professors, numbering about 2,400 and emphasizing stronger insurance programs. Then there is the California College and University Faculty Association, which is an offshoot of the politically powerful California Teachers Association. Most of the education faculty members belong to this organization. The California State Employees Association, which includes all public employees, has local state college chapters. This group and the American Association of University Professors are apparently the least militant.

In short, the California master plan is in deep trouble, and the state colleges are at the center of the agitation. Meanwhile, the Legislative Joint Committee on Higher Education has its own scheme. This committee believes that the present layer-cake structure of public and private institutions is an obstacle to effective planning and distribution of resources in all the areas where the legislature has concerns: budgeting, equal-opportunity programs, faculty supply, admission policies, capital outlay programs, for example. This committee wants to restructure the system to provide some means of statewide planning tied together with regional planning and program implementation that would enable the junior colleges, state colleges, university, and private institutions to work together. The complaint is that each segment now seems to operate largely as if none of the others exists; each is said to try to feather its own nest financially in direct competition rather than coordination. This amounts to an indictment of the effectiveness of the Coordinating Council, the voluntary nature of which perhaps doomed it from the start. Greatly concerned about the skyrocketing costs, the legislature views the future development of the state colleges, in particular, with trepidation. In the eyes of some legislators, the alternative to regional development would seem to be a second university system composed of state colleges, entailing vast additional costs, duplication of effort, and increased competition for resources.

The education community has reacted negatively to the joint committee's proposal for reorganization, feeling generally that the regional-center idea would create a more cumbersome system than exists at present. It would enhance the role of the legislature when budgets are presented because of the dilution effect of replacing the present boards for the university and state colleges and community colleges with five or more regional centers.

One could do a whole book on the California situation, complex as it is. The issues in California do point up the very tricky relationship between local demands for autonomy and initiative and the need for a systems approach at the state level for the proper allocation of resources. It does seem that an inordinate and crippling set of bureaucratic controls besets the state colleges—pre- and postauditing of a 27,000-line-item budget and silly out-of-state travel regulations, for example. Apparently, many of these petty controls originated with the state budget office but have now been transferred to the chancellor's office, where, according to many faculty and administrators, they still continue.

A great deal more discretion at the institutional level in expenditure of funds is called for by both faculty and administrators since the colleges differ considerably in program emphasis and style. Cal Poly at San Luis Obispo emphasizes applied occupational programs, specifically middle-level engineering. Chico, on the other hand, is rapidly becoming a liberal arts college. San Francisco State is in sharp contrast to both with its cosmopolitanism and sophistication, together with professional emphasis on the arts and humanities. Cal State at Los Angeles is a lusty commuter college. Humboldt State, on the redwood coastline, with its curricula in areas such as marine biology and lumber, appeals to a different kind of student. San Diego, until recently the only major public institution in the area, has something for just about everybody.

NEW YORK Just as California has taken over the population lead from New York, so the Empire State has ambitions to overtake California in higher education. Though the State University of New York (SUNY) system was established in 1948, only recently have the enormous strides been taken that many hope will make New York number one in the country in higher education. The most fundamental difference between the New York and California systems is that SUNY has a single board of trustees overseeing the entire system of some 67 universities, colleges, and other special centers. There are not separate boards for the university and the state colleges, as in California. The single board, with its chancellor, Samuel Gould, coordinates the entire operation and presents a single budget to the legislature. All the presidents of the SUNY institutions, from the smallest community college to the largest university center, have direct access to the chancellor, though for practical purposes many of them deal directly with the particular dean in the central office specifically associated with their kind of institution. In practice, what this means is that usually the presidents from the university centers and a few of the state colleges deal directly with the chancellor while, for example, many of the community college presidents negotiate directly with the community college dean.

In the background, of course, is the New York State Board of Regents with the commissioner of education as its chief executive officer. In theory, the regents exercise control over *both* public and private schools and colleges throughout New York State. This means that the SUNY board of trustees has basically the same relationship with the regents as, for example, the boards of Columbia or Colgate. The SUNY master plan, redone every four years, must be approved by the regents; otherwise, the operation of the SUNY system is left to the chancellor and the individual institutions.

The general feeling seems to be that relationships between the individual institutions and the central office in Albany are still being worked out, and one cannot be sure just where lines will ultimately be drawn between institutional autonomy and central control. Because none of the positions is as yet fixed, there is not the restiveness, indeed outspoken bitterness, in New York that one finds on state college campuses in California. Although New York state college faculty members face the same prohibitions against university status and doctoral degrees as the state college faculty in California, their morale is much higher.

The difference may be accounted for in two ways. First, the decision against doctoral degrees at the state colleges has been a legislative one in California; in New York this has been a decision of the SUNY board of trustees. The feeling seems to be that a board decision is easier to change than legislation. Indeed, as we saw at Brockport, faculty are being hired with the lure that doctoral programs and university status are just around the corner. The second reason lies in the novelty of the whole system, including the universities. Just a few years ago New York State had no public university; California has had great pride for many years in the University of California. Consequently, the state college faculty in New York do not feel like second-class citizens alongside the faculty of well-established, prestigious universities.

NEW JERSEY New Jersey has been called a disaster area in higher education for many years. Although one of the wealthiest states in the nation, its per capita expenditures in higher education have been the lowest in the nation. Over 50 percent of New Jersey youths wanting higher education must go outside the state. Only recently has Rutgers become a full-fledged state university. The six state colleges, despite their name change from teachers colleges back in 1958, remain to this day very much single-purpose, teacher training institutions.

The state colleges had been under the thumb of the state department of education and its board, so much so that actual department enrollments at the state colleges were dictated by teacher demand in the public schools. Incoming students were forced to sign a pledge that they would teach in New Jersey schools. The

combination of control by the education authorities and fiscal star-
vation held New Jersey state colleges years behind development in
other, more progressive states, especially in the Midwest and Far
West.

Governor Richard Hughes, with the assistance of a blue-ribbon
citizens committee headed by Pres. Robert Goheen of Princeton,
pushed hard for reform, and the legislature passed the Higher
Education Act of 1966. This created a separate department of
higher education and a board of higher education. Ralph Dungan,
one of the Kennedy men in the White House, was plucked from his
ambassadorship in Chile to become the first chancellor.

The first year's operation of the new department was a rough one.
The Dungan appointment smacked of politics to many of the state
college people who were not consulted about his selection; and
these same people reacted as one might expect toward what appeared to be criticisms of the state colleges from the chancellor's
office—criticism that alienated the very people whose support was
needed most. Presidencies of several of the state colleges became
vacant. Sharp controversy ensued after a state board policy decision that eliminated the departmental quota system for admission, thereby raising admission standards in the six colleges. Cries
of "elitism" arose, and many felt that schoolteachers for the elementary grades, physical education, and the nonacademic secondary
subjects would soon be in short supply.

At the same time, the promise of much better things to come as
a result of the new structure and a new state sales tax was undercut
when the opposition party swept the statewide elections. Not only
have state college faculty been upset, but students at the six colleges have taken up the battle and indeed have marched on the
capitol building in Trenton, holding a mock funeral procession
for the state colleges. So, by the close of 1968, there seemed to be
growing support for the chancellor, the target of the students and
faculty having shifted somewhat to the legislature.

A bond issue for capital funds proposed by a special governor's
advisory committee and the board of higher education was cut
back by the legislature in 1968. Also reduced was the operating
budget that had been approved by the chancellor's office for 1968-
1969. In fact, the legislature dictated a specific salary schedule
within the appropriations bill. Nevertheless, in its annual report
on faculty salaries, the AAUP extended kudos to the New Jersey
state colleges for a dramatic increase over the two-year period

1967-1969. In terms of a percentage increase, they are in the top 5 percent of the nation; their faculties (now aggressively organizing under the powerful New Jersey Education Association) are at the B+ level on the AAUP scale. This has been made possible by a 44 percent increase in state appropriations for operating expenses over the two-year period.

Though salaries have gone up impressively, financial problems remain if the system is to expand. The situation at Trenton State illustrates the problems. Existing programs are understaffed and underfinanced, and the current enrollment of 4,300 students does not come close to meeting the demands for places. In 1968 there were 5,400 applicants and 1,500 were admitted.

Another problem for administrators, students, and faculty alike has been the lack of fiscal autonomy for the colleges. Legislation has been passed to improve this situation. The state colleges, like those in California, have had a line-item budget as contrasted to both the state university and the community colleges, and this has meant an incredible amount of bureaucratic control, especially from the state budget office, making questionable the efficient operation of the state colleges and in particular the authority of the local boards of trustees and administrators.

The new state board of higher education has jurisdiction over the newly developing community colleges as well as the state colleges. Its relationship to Rutgers, the state university, still remains somewhat cloudy. The goal of the board is to encourage as much institutional autonomy as possible consistent with sensible state-wide coordination and planning. Unlike New York, where the local institutional boards have been window dressing in the past, the object in New Jersey is to have the newly created state college boards exercise real initiative and leadership in developing the local institutions. One of the obvious problems of the first year was that the new boards had not as yet dug into their jobs while at the same time the chancellor's office demanded action. This gave the appearance, in the eyes of some, of excessive control from Trenton. Whatever the system, the balance between autonomy and control is intricate. The problem in New Jersey is how the chancellor's office can stimulate action without being coercive toward institutions which have never had much autonomy—all within a new system with as yet vaguely defined relationships among the community colleges, state colleges, and university.

One area of concern is institutional purpose. Eastern state colleges seem more oriented toward the traditional liberal arts than colleges elsewhere and correspondingly less oriented toward professional and occupational programs. There is a narrower range of academic respectability in the major Eastern universities, which are private, than in the major Western universities, which are public. And the colleges tend to model themselves after the universities. This question of institutional model has been an issue in the New Jersey state colleges. The state board apparently had been calling loosely for the emergence of liberal arts colleges, whereas some of the college people insisted upon the phrase *multipurpose colleges*. The difference is highly significant because the latter name suggests a variety of vocationally oriented and professional programs on top of a liberal arts base, whereas the former would seem to eliminate anything with a vocational bent. The Higher Education Act of 1966 refers to "higher education in the liberal arts and sciences and various professional areas including the science of education and the art of teaching. . . ."

The influence of private higher education is pervasive. Many of the large number of students turned away by the state colleges for lack of space go to New Jersey private institutions since out-of-state public colleges have cut down on New Jersey residents. For this reason, the private colleges (about 25) have prospered and, aside from Princeton, which is not threatened by the public institutions, appear to take a dim view of the necessary development of public higher education, principally the state colleges. Up to now, the public has felt the same way. There has been in New Jersey, as in many Eastern states, something of a disbelief that public colleges can be any good. Upper-class commuters who send their children to private schools and colleges share this view with northern New Jersey Catholics who send their children to parochial schools and then to Seton Hall or St. Peter's. Naturally, they want to keep taxes down. The horrendously low per capita support of public higher education has been the result. There has been in the past just enough support to provide an outlet for lower-middle-class children to go to college and then back into the public schools to take care of more lower-middle-class children.

Aside from New York, there is just no question that, in general, the East lags behind the Midwest and Far West in developing public higher education. This basic difference is illustrated by Virgil W. Gillenwater, former president of Trenton State. Gillenwater had come to New Jersey with high expectations of engaging himself in the exciting development of the state colleges, much as he had been involved in the development of public higher education in Illinois and Arizona. Having been president of Trenton State for slightly over a year, he resigned to return to Northern Arizona University.

He had brought with him to New Jersey a total commitment to public higher education, a typically Western view. He did not find this; instead he found a typical Eastern view—namely, a strong commitment to private education at both the school and college level. He was irritated by people who seemed amazed that he sent his children to public schools. Gillenwater's position on the role of state colleges perhaps is best revealed by his feeling that an ideal admissions policy would be to accept anyone from the top half of the high school graduating class; he takes umbrage at Eastern notions of selectivity and exclusiveness and believes that SAT scores are irrelevant to the mission of a state college. I hazard the generalization that more state college administrators than not support and, in fact, applaud this viewpoint. Whether their new breed faculty—and New Jersey legislators—agree is another matter! Meanwhile, Gillenwater's academically oriented successor found himself in deep trouble with his faculty in late spring 1969.

ILLINOIS   In Illinois, most of the four-year public institutions are called universities though the institutions range along the spectrum at every level of development from single-purpose teacher training to multi-purpose university. Southern Illinois University, a teachers college not long ago, is now one of the largest universities in the country and clearly belongs at the far right of the spectrum of development. As far as governance is concerned, Illinois represents still another pattern. It is in sharpest contrast, perhaps, to California, where specific rules and functions for institutions are delineated by the legislature. In Illinois there is no predetermination, so that theoretically any institution can offer any program. In short, there is no brake on institutional ambition—perhaps university status for all! There is a collection of at least five systems and boards, all held together by a strong coordinating mechanism in the form of the state board of higher education.

OHIO AND MAINE   The pattern in Ohio has been entirely different. There, when a concern for teacher education became pronounced at the turn of the century, the established institutions created their own normal schools, which later became colleges of education within Ohio University, Miami University, and Ohio State University. Two additional teachers colleges were established, which have now become Kent State University and Bowling Green State University. A problem in Ohio has been to decide the extent and scope of doctoral programs at the universities; each place apparently has ambitions to duplicate Ohio State. On top of this kind of problem sits the Ohio Board of Regents in Columbus. Perhaps the major problem that board has been wrestling with in the 1960s has been to develop a relationship between the public universities and the centers of urban population. The municipal universities—Akron, Cincinnati, and Toledo—have become, in effect, state universities for this purpose. In addition, new state universities have been created in Cleveland, Dayton, and Youngstown.

Still another pattern is in Maine, where the five state colleges and the state university have been brought together into a single system known as the University of Maine. The system is headed by a chancellor, with presidents on each of the campuses.

NORTH CAROLINA The story of the transformation of the state colleges in North Carolina to regional universities would make an excellent book for a musical comedy—Gilbert and Sullivan could have done a beautiful job with a plot so thoroughly entangled that an out-of-stater finds himself helpless in trying to understand what really happened. The leading character in the story is Leo W. Jenkins, the energetic and ambitious president of East Carolina College in Greenville. A mixture of academic entrepreneur and adroit politician, he parlayed a set of complicated issues into a drive for university status for his college. With the help of former Gov. Terry Sanford, he got that status, not just for his own institution but for three others as well. That the others were brought along, which was not President Jenkins' idea, may well blunt the ambitions of East Carolina, diluting the effect of the university name when it comes time for state appropriations.

The debate involved all kinds of issues and emotions: the status and name of North Carolina State University, the failure of the system of higher education to serve the eastern part of the state, Leo Jenkins' ambitions for his institution and perhaps for himself (the governorship), the combination of political forces entwined around the infamous speaker-ban controversy, racism, and broad-based Populism. The University of North Carolina was the symbol of elitism and liberalism. Wooing the people, Leo Jenkins made hundreds of speeches throughout the state; he knew every legislator by first name and still carries a directory with their names and pictures. He was successful and carried the day against the recommendation of the North Carolina Board of Higher Education.

The politicking meant a terrible embroglio around the state—and all over a name. What disturbs some observers about what took place is the lack of attention paid to overall state needs in higher education, the lack of planning and coordination that was supposedly the role of the board of higher education, and most important, political activity that bypassed the educational community. Observers say that now higher education in North Carolina is a political football, with legislators moving in on every side as a result of the fiasco of July 1, 1967. Recriminations and talk of scandal at East Carolina University still make good newspaper copy, especially in the liberal Raleigh papers. Critics of Leo Jenkins admit his shrewdness in political matters but berate his naïveté in educational matters, claiming that he makes no distinction between quantity and quality and probably doesn't know the difference. His supporters point to what he has done for his institution and the eastern part of the state. So East Carolina University today remains a center of controversy. Meanwhile, its programs and enrollments continue to expand dramatically as it strives to reach out to the people of eastern North Carolina. It is a place to be reckoned with.

For the past few years, the American Council on Education has had under way a study of statewide systems of education, directed by Robert Berdahl. A questionnaire was sent to state university and state college presidents asking about the locus of decision making within their states. The presidents were asked to identify the role of the institution, the state coordinating agency if one exists, and the state government in relation to 47 specific areas of decision making. They were also asked to indicate their opinion as to what the respective roles of the three interested parties should be.

The direction of responses implied greater independence and self-assuredness among the university presidents than among the state college presidents. Take the matter of assigning purposes and functions to institutions: in states with no coordinating councils, 68 percent of the university presidents felt that the institution should define its role but only 44 percent of the college presidents felt the same way. Regardless of the state structure, with questions such as admission standards, enrollment, and out-of-state student quotas, a higher percentage of university presidents than college presidents consistently opted for institutional prerogatives. This lack of self-assertiveness among the state college presidents shows up in responses to a question on general policies affecting the rights of faculty to engage in partisan politics. The state college presidents were not willing to go as far as the university presidents in desiring to reduce the authority of the state in the hiring, promotion, and salaries of top administrators. In general, then, the state college presidents seemed considerably more deferential toward state boards and coordinating councils than did the university presidents. The difference may well be due to the traditional ties of state colleges to state departments of education and the relative lack of autonomy that these ties mean. But once they are broken, as in New Jersey and New York, the situation can change rapidly, especially with enrollment growth and proportionately more Ph.D's on the faculty.

4. The Financing of State Colleges, Broadway Theater, and Gourmet Restaurants

What does higher education have in common with Broadway theater and gourmet restaurants? Anyone who recently has had dinner in New York and then gone to the theater and has paid college tuition knows the answer: high cost. In these activities the costs are rising far faster than living costs in general. William Bowen, economist and provost at Princeton, has looked at the financial future of both the performing arts and higher education. Both are in trouble. The nub of the problem is the inability of these segments of the economy to increase their productivity. Higher wages for auto workers are offset by technological advance and greater car production, with the result that the wage increases are not simply passed along to the fellow who buys a car. On the other hand, higher wages for college professors (their wages have gone up dramatically in the past several years) or for actors or oboe players are not offset by a corresponding increase in the number of students taught or the number of plays performed. These costs are passed along to the consumer. Car prices go up but not nearly so fast as the price of a theater ticket or a college education. Costs would go up even if the educational enterprise stood still, but the expansion of higher education in all directions — students, faculty, research, expensive graduate programs, new areas of study, buildings — compounds the problem immensely. So far, there have not been dramatic technological breakthroughs in education that enable a cut in costs while preserving the personal student-teacher relationship many feel is crucial to the educational process. Costs soar, especially at the upper-division and graduate levels. The price tag is something like 20 times greater for a Ph.D. in physics than it is for a freshman.

First-class graduate work is done on an apprentice basis, almost a one-to-one relationship between student and professor. The assumption among academicians is that this highly costly tradition cannot be changed without sacrificing quality. This may be true, yet I wonder if the assumption has been seriously examined. From a social-benefit viewpoint, a case could be made that a slum child in a first-grade class with 30 or 40 others needs more individual attention than a 23-year-old graduate student. It seems somehow strange that we spend the least money on young children who don't know anything and the most money on young adults who think they know everything! What is especially bothersome, almost fraudulent,

TABLE 11 *Estimated current-funds revenues of state colleges and universities by purpose and source, fiscal year 1965-66 (dollars in thousands)*

				Purpose
	Educational and general			
Source	*All except organized research and organized activities*	*Organized research*	*Organized activities relating to educational departments*	*Student-aid grants*
Total current-funds revenues	$1,153,958	$42,885	$47,422	$31,013
Tuition and fees	248,263	280	5,328	3,982
Room, board, and all other charges to individual users of services	3,498	9	7,290	223
Earnings from endowment investment	1,435	220	4	493
Private gifts and grants	5,499	5,647	770	4,499
Local government	10,379	542	1,329	57
State government	833,883	9,135	13,247	14,261
Federal government	35,287	26,457	14,050	6,778
Other sources	15,714	595	5,404	720
Percent distribution of state colleges and universities total	69	3	3	2
Percent distribution of total U.S.	57	19	5	2
Percent distribution of U.S. public	60	17	5	2
Percent of total U.S.	16	2	8	1
Percent of U.S. public	26	4	13	2

SOURCE: Compiled by Carnegie Commission on Higher Education from U.S. Office of Education data.

is the way in which the enormous per pupil costs of graduate instruction are passed along to taxpayers and parents in the form of higher tuition for undergraduates. What *is* fraudulent is the fact that the unsuspecting taxpayer and parent willingly supports higher education in the belief that the soaring costs will be reflected in better-quality instruction for his freshman son. In prestigious universities, faculty salaries are constantly bid up either to recruit or to protect faculty members who spend little time with undergraduates. I vividly recall a dinner given in honor of a Nobel laureate, who

Auxiliary enterprises			*Percent distribution*			*Percent of*	
Housing and food service	*All other*	*Total*	*State colleges and universities*	*Total U.S.*	*U.S. public*	*Total U.S.*	*U.S. public*
$257,835	$128,079	$1,661,192	100	100	100	13	22
1,099	5,965	264,917	16	22	12	10	30
250,333	103,085	364,438	22	16	16	17	22
171	80	2,403		3	1	1	6
17	3,282	19,714	1	6	3	3	10
8	27	12,342	1	2	4	4	4
3,852	363	874,741	53	24	40	29	29
771	578	83,921	5	22	19	3	6
1,584	14,699	38,716	2	5	5	5	10
15	8	100					
10	7	100					
9	7	100					
20	15	13					
39	23	22					

described his genuine affection for his students to an appreciative trustee audience. Little did many of the beaming trustees realize that he was referring to his graduate students; he hadn't had much to do with undergraduates for years.

In any case, because of the enormous cost of graduate education, it is understandable that the established universities and state-wide boards look with great concern at ambitious state colleges wishing to take on university status. With that university status come inevitably a desire for doctoral programs and, just as inevitably, vast increases in expenditures to maintain a very low student-teacher ratio at the graduate level and to provide the highly expensive facilities, equipment, and library for advanced work.

TABLE 12 *Estimated current-funds expenditures of state colleges and universities by function and source, fiscal year 1965-66 (dollars in thousands)*

		Percent distribution			Percent of	
	Amount	*State colleges and universities*	*Total U.S.*	*U.S. public*	*Total U.S.*	*U.S. public*
Total expenditures	$1,553,892	100	100	100	12	22
Total educational and general	1,148,375	74	80	81	12	20
Instruction and departmental research	653,290	42	30	33	17	27
Extension and public service	26,087	2	4	6	6	7
Libraries	64,645	4	3	3	19	32
Physical-plant maintenance and operation	134,943	9	7	7	16	27
General administration	162,173	11	10	9	13	26
Organized activities relating to educational departments	36,890	2	4	5	7	11
Organized research	37,019	2	20	16	2	3
Other sponsored activities.	12,613	1	1	1	8	12
All others	20,715	1	1	1	13	19
Student-aid grants	33,402	2	3	2	8	21
Total auxiliary enterprises	338,082	22	15	15	18	32
Housing and food services	215,780	14	9	8	19	38
Other	122,302	8	6	7	16	25
Current funds for physical-plant assets	34,033	2	2	2	14	29

SOURCE: Compiled by Carnegie Commission on Higher Education from U.S. Office of Education data.

Additional money going to a regional university to inaugurate a doctoral program may well mean less money going to the state university for its programs. Again, the issue: institutional autonomy and development alongside state planning and control with limited financial resources.

There is another interesting angle to the drive toward university status. In some states it has meant, ironically, playing upon current anti-intellectualism aimed at the major state university. Populist appeals to regional and local prejudices result often in more money and in university status from the state legislature. The liberal state university, with all its cosmopolitanism and national flavor, is painted as the devil, and the regional state college, the people's college, reaps the rewards.

INCOME AND EXPENDITURES But let's return to the problems of finance. Readers with a penchant for budgets can have fun wallowing in an abundance of state college statistics. Tables 11 to 17 have been specially put together by the Carnegie Commission from the massive Higher Education General Information Survey of the U.S. Office of Education for 1965 - 66. Though now somewhat out of date, they are the most comprehensive data that have been assembled for AASCU institutions. Aggregate figures are compared to all of higher education and to all public colleges and universities.

As one might expect, state funds are the primary source—just over half (53 percent)—of current revenue in AASCU colleges. Room and board charges are second (22 percent), and tuition and fees third (16 percent). The figures are different for *all* public institutions: state funds, 40 percent; federal funds, 19 percent; room and board, 16 percent; and tuition and fees, 12 percent. The difference is due primarily to the influence of federal research funds in the major public universities. Seventeen percent of the revenues in *all* public institutions is for organized research; the figure is only 3 percent in AASCU institutions.

On the expenditure side, the emphasis upon teaching is apparent. Forty-two percent of the educational and general funds are spent on instruction, in contrast to 33 percent in all public institutions. The rest of the expenditure pattern is similar to other public institutions except that the state colleges spend relatively little on organized research and relatively more on housing and food services. It is interesting that the state colleges also spend relatively a bit more on libraries than other public institutions, but less on extension services.

TABLE 13
*Estimated
capital funds
receipts of
state colleges
and
universities by
source and fund,
fiscal year
1965 - 66
(dollars in
thousands)*

	Physical-plant funds	Endowment funds
Total capital funds receipts	$402,176	$1,523
Fees charged to students	36,045	6
Receipts added to funds from investment of funds	3,292	152
Private gifts and grants	855	589
Local governments	1,313	
State governments	224,343	
Federal government	115,846	
Other sources	20,482	776
Percent distribution of total	99	
Percent distribution of total U.S.	76	21
Percent distribution of U.S. public	91	7
Percent of total U.S.	21	
Percent of U S. public	30	1

SOURCE: Compiled by Carnegie Commission on Higher Education from U.S. Office of Education data.

TABLE 14   *Estimated capital funds loans received by state colleges and universities by source and fund, fiscal year 1965 - 66 (dollars in thousands)*

		Physical-plant funds		
		Percent distribution		
	Amount	State colleges and universities	Total U.S.	U.S. public
Total capital funds borrowed during the year	$430,970	100	100	100
Other funds of the institution	3,231	1	5	2
Private sources outside the institution	152,861	35	43	48
Local government			4	6
State government	174,571	41	21	24
Federal government	100,307	23	27	20
Percent of total U.S.	27			
Percent of U.S. public	43			

SOURCE: Compiled by Carnegie Commission on Higher Education from U.S. Office of Education data.

Annuity and [l]ving [tr]ust [fu]nds	Student-loan funds	Total	Percent distribution			Percent of	
			State colleges and universities	Total U.S.	U.S. public	Total U.S.	U.S. public
$7	$3,569	$407,275	100	100	100	16	28
	418	36,469	9	4	6	35	42
1	240	3,685	1	10	5	1	5
6	541	1,991	1	28	7		2
	34	1,347		3	5	2	2
	1,167	225,510	55	30	50	30	31
	550	116,396	29	13	18	35	44
	619	21,877	5	12	9	7	16
	1	100					
2	1	100					
1	1	100					
	14	16					
	31	28					

Percent of		Student-loan funds						
			Percent distribution			Percent of		
[To]tal [U.]S.	U.S. public	Amount	State colleges and universities	Total U.S.	U.S. public	Total U.S.	U.S. public	Total amount
[1]7	43	$46,095	100	100	100	22	45	$477,065
4	17	1,619	3	3	4	25	42	4,850
22	32	242	1	1	1	22	43	153,103
52	71	757	2	1	1	32	66	175,328
24	50	43,477	94	95	94	22	45	143,784
		22						
		45						

When we compare current revenues and expenditures, the state colleges are in the black; revenues exceed expenditures by 6.9 percent, in comparison with 4 percent in all public institutions. The state colleges apparently make more money on what little research they do than other public colleges, and they do better on housing and food services. All in all, the state colleges are doing rather well in regard to current funds compared with all public institutions.

When it comes to capital funds, state colleges receive 55 percent from the state and 29 percent from federal sources, which is a higher figure than for all public institutions. Almost all the money goes for physical-plant needs. Forty-one percent of the physical-plant loans come from the states, 35 percent from private sources, and 23 percent from federal sources. The state colleges get relatively much more in loans from the states than do other public institutions; in fact, they absorb 71 percent of all state physical-plant loans going to public colleges. Like most other colleges, state college student-loan funds come from the federal government. Fifty

TABLE 15
Estimated federal funds disbursed by state colleges and universities, fiscal year 1965 - 66 (dollars in thousands)

	Department of HEW			
Funds expended by purpose	USOE	PHS	Other HEW	DO
Grants and contracts:				
Instruction and departmental research	$ 6,151	$ 979	$1,817	$ 2
Extension and public service	206	93	255	
Organized research	1,516	1,469	353	7
Other sponsored activities	3,549	256	409	
Libraries	414	6	12	
Student financial aid	19,425	1,185	706	8
Physical-plant facilities	7,764	36	650	
Other grants and contracts	857	6	451	
TOTAL	39,882	4,030	4,653	13
Percent	50	5	6	
Loans: Student-loan funds	41,224	128	426	
Physical facilities Other loans	15			
TOTAL	41,239	128	426	
Percent	39			

SOURCE: Compiled by Carnegie Commission on Higher Education from U.S. Office of Education data.

percent of student grants came from the federal government, in comparison with 42 percent at other public institutions. What the state colleges do not share in very much are programs sponsored by agencies or departments other than the U.S. Office of Education.

All the federal funds disbursed by state colleges break down as follows: $79.4 million in grants and contracts and $106.6 million in loans. Twenty-five percent of the grants and contracts are for instruction, 13 percent for other sponsored activities, 28 percent for student aid, 18 percent for physical plant, and only 9 percent for organized research. Fifty percent of these grants and contracts come from the U.S. Office of Education. Loan funds are split 61 percent for physical facilities (mostly from the Department of Housing and Urban Development) and 39 percent for student loans, almost all from the Office of Education.

THE FINANCIAL PINCH In looking over state college presidents' replies to a questionnaire on the problems of finance, sent out in the summer of 1967 by Editorial Projects for Education (EPE), I was struck by the extent to

DOD	HUD	AEC	NASA	NSF	All other	Total	Percent
639		$ 40	$ 22	$ 4,179	$ 5,603	$ 19,455	25
8				28	518	1,108	1
449	$8	224	572	2,070	793	7,531	9
33		16	13	2,883	2,841	10,000	13
			3	37	41	513	1
		12	58	521	600	22,537	28
	4,386	40		1,162	11	14,049	18
11		14	33	506	2,307	4,185	5
1,140	4,394	346	701	11,386	12,714	79,378	100
2	6		1	14	16	100	
24				23		41,825	39
1,286	63,478					64,764	61
						15	
1,310	63,478			23		106,604	100
1	60					100	

which many did not feel a severe financial strain. Public institutions are not allowed to operate at a deficit. The state colleges use black ink; revenues exceed expenditures. State funds have been forthcoming; the institutions are not about to fold up. But what happens is that worthwhile new programs are deferred from year to year for lack of funds. Time and again, the replies from the state college presidents made the point that planned program expansion could not take place because of inadequate funding at the state level. State legislatures have, for the most part, been willing to provide funds for current programs, increased enrollments, and

TABLE 16 *Estimated student financial aid funds disbursed by state colleges and universities by type of program, type of aid, and academic level of recipient, fiscal year 1965-66 (dollars in thousands)*

	Type of program		
	Nonfederally sponsored	Federally sponsored	
		U.S. Office of Education	
Type of student financial aid and academic level of recipient		Nonfederal matching funds	Federal funds
Work assignments:			
Undergraduate	$23,848	$1,972	$17,309
First professional	10		
Graduate	4,016	87	1,169
Total work assignments	27,874	2,059	18,478
Grants:			
Undergraduate	26,188	23	1,719
First professional	15		
Graduate	3,405	5	1,018
Total grants	29,608	28	2,737
Loans:			
Undergraduate	5,422	4,847	43,971
First professional	39	8	73
Graduate	275	278	2,397
Total loans	5,736	5,133	46,261
TOTAL	63,218	7,220	67,476
Percent distribution state colleges and universities	45	5	48
Percent distribution total U.S.	56	3	28
Percent distribution U.S. public	54	3	31
Percent of total U.S.	11	24	24
Percent of U.S. public	23	44	43

SOURCE: Compiled by Carnegie Commission on Higher Education from U.S. Office of Education data.

salary boosts. (I shall discuss faculty salaries in a later chapter.) Funds are usually made available on the basis of formulas into which are fed projected enrollment figures. This procedure does not allow, for example, a new computer program, those experimental freshmen seminars, or special programs for the disadvantaged. In many states another major problem is meshing institutional long-range planning and budget development with legislative time schedules. This has been a very serious problem at the federal level as well.

That the states are responsive at least to the enrollment and

| *her federal partments and agencies* | | | *Percent distribution* | | | *Percent of* | |
Nonfederal matching funds	*Federal funds*	*Total all funds*	*State colleges and universities*	*Total U.S.*	*U.S. public*	*Total U.S.*	*U.S. public*
$118	$1,262	$44,509	31	22	30	20	29
		10		1			
6	163	5,441	4	8	12	6	9
124	1,425	49,960	35	31	42	16	23
	721	28,651	20	25	17	11	35
	83	98		2	1	1	2
	1,039	5,467	4	14	13	4	8
	1,843	34,216	24	41	31	8	22
13	132	54,205	38	22	22	24	49
2	22	144		2	2	1	2
28	249	3,227	3	4	3	9	17
43	403	57,576	41	28	27	20	41
167	3,671	141,752	100	100	100	14	28
	2	100					
	13	100					
	11	100					
8	3	14					
22	6	28					

salary pressures in higher education is illustrated by an extraordinary 40 percent increase in operating funds in the two-year period 1966-1968. In Michigan, for example, Northern Michigan University has had its appropriations increased by 35 percent in two years, Eastern Michigan University by 37 percent—in contrast to the University of Michigan with 9 percent and Michigan State University and Western Michigan with 12 percent. New York State figures have been until now even more astounding. Brockport

TABLE 17 *Estimated physical-plant fixed assets of state colleges and universities by beginning and ending values, additions and deductions during the year, total and type of asset, fiscal year 1965-66 (dollars in thousands)*

Balance and transaction	Land	Improve-ment	Buildings
Book value of plant fixed assets at beginning of fiscal year	$198,631	$153,724	$2,964,898
Additions to plant fixed assets during year			
By expenditures	28,664	14,240	480,916
By gift-in-kind from donor	890	97	5,777
By reappraisal of plant value	710	14	10,957
By other additions	679	347	21,342
Total additions during the year	30,343	14,698	518,992
Deduction from plant fixed assets during year	914	64	7,623
Book value of plant fixed assets at ending of fiscal year	228,660	168,358	3,476,267
Percent distribution state colleges and universities additions during year	5	2	82
Percent distribution total U.S. additions during year	6	3	71
Percent distribution U.S. public additions during year	6	4	69
Percent of total U.S. additions	18	13	23
Percent of U.S. public additions	26	19	38
Percent of book value of plant fixed assets at ending of fiscal year	13	18	18
Percent of U.S. public book value of plant fixed assets at ending of year	26	23	31

SOURCE: Compiled by Carnegie Commission on Higher Education from U.S. Office of Education data.

and New Paltz show increases of 51 percent, and the rest of the established state colleges are almost as high. In California, the University of California shows a two-year increase of 21 percent, while the state colleges show an increase in operating funds of 36 percent.

"Serious, but not critical"—this would seem to sum up the financial predicament of the state colleges and universities. They appear not to be in nearly so severe straits as many of the private

		Percent distribution			Percent of	
ipment	*Total*	*State colleges and universities*	*Total U.S.*	*U.S. public*	*Total U.S.*	*U.S. public*
17,394	$3,834,647				16	28
65,543	589,363	93	91	93	21	32
2,170	8,934	1	2	1	12	31
1,319	13,000	2	2	2	18	29
1,009	23,377	4	5	4	17	33
70,041	634,674	100	100	100	20	32
4,728	13,329				9	17
32,707	4,455,992				17	28
11	100					
20	100					
21	100					
11	20					
17	32					
13	17					
20	28					

institutions. Interestingly, in response to a question on the EPE 1967 questionnaire about whether federal support is the only realistic solution to the financial problem, the state college presidents reacted somewhat negatively to federal aid as the most effective cure. Most have had some bad experience with federal aid programs, bureaucracy, and the like. Moreover, the state college presidents are very sensitive to the fact that many of the categorical aid programs at the federal level, especially in research, simply do not help them but go instead to the already established private and state universities. There is something of a sour taste in the mouths of many state college people when federal programs come up for discussion. Whether these people are realistic in expecting state support to expand greatly is another matter. I would say that state college presidents look more to the state than to the federal government for financial help—despite the very strong stand for increased federal aid taken by AASCU in conjunction with NASULGC.

Actually, between 1963 and 1966 the total amount of federal support to state colleges went up by a factor of 6, according to National Science Foundation (NSF) figures. In comparison with the rest of higher education, state colleges in 1963 received only 2.2 percent of the federal largess that year; they received 7.5 percent of the total in 1966. Federal nonscience support in the three-year period rose from 4.4 percent to 16.9 percent of the total, but state college spokesmen don't like the fact that in 1966 their institutions received only 3.7 percent of federal funds for academic science. Whereas only 63 percent of the AASCU colleges received some federal support in 1963, by 1966 virtually all the colleges received some federal funds, with the science support concentrated, as one would expect, at the larger institutions.

ENDOWMENT AND TUITION

Just a word about endowment income and revenues from tuition. In 1966 endowment income amounted to less than 1 percent of current revenue in state colleges, only 1 percent in all public higher education, 3 percent overall in higher education. A different investment policy with an emphasis on growth stocks and spending out of capital gains may help private colleges somewhat; it won't help much in the public institutions, especially the state colleges, where endowments are so meager to begin with. Typical alumni of state colleges, schoolteachers, are not likely to leave their alma maters large bequests, nor are they likely to contribute large sums to annual fund drives. My impression, nevertheless, is that very little concerted effort has been made to seek out private funds in general, alumni funds in particular.

I noted earlier that tuition accounts for only 16 percent of the current revenue in state colleges. In 1969 - 1970, the average charge for tuition and fees is $350, a 14 percent increase in one year (Table 18). The total budget for an in-state student is about $1,400 after $832 is added for room and board and $200 for books, laundry, and incidentals. As high as the $1,400 figure is, it is still less than one-third the annual budget required at many of the major private liberal arts colleges. As we shall see later, there is no doubt that low cost is a large factor in the decision of many students to attend a state college.

There is no doubt either that low tuition is an article of faith in state colleges, as it is in all public higher education. It is also an issue of tremendous concern to private colleges as the gap widens between their charges and those at the public institutions. Much of the opposition to federal aid proposals which would aid students rather than institutions is that this would force tuition charges higher at public colleges. Generally, the feeling in public higher education is that the financial burden for higher education should be borne by society, just as the cost of public schools is borne by the public at large. Society is said to be the primary beneficiary of a well-educated populace; therefore society, not the individual, should pick up the tab. Higher education becomes a right, not a

TABLE 18
Student tuition and other fees in AASCU member institutions

	1968 - 69	*1969 - 70*
In-state tuition fees	$307	$350
Out-of-state tuition fees	716	788
Room rate (men)	288	330
Room rate (women)	291	332
Board rate (men)	420	441
Board rate (women)	420	441
*Combined room and board (men)**	790	832
*Combined room and board (women)**	790	832

*Combined rate reported by some institutions.
SOURCE: *The Chronicle of Higher Education,* vol. IV, no. 1, p. 1, Sept. 29, 1969.

privilege. The argument on the other side is that the student obviously benefits greatly from higher education: his income goes up, and he leads a qualitatively better life. He, therefore, should pay the cost. Besides, he is likely to take his education more seriously if he has a financial stake in it. (This reasoning often leads to the dubious conclusion that higher student charges will reduce campus strife. White activists tend to come from affluent families, and many pay full tuition at high-cost private universities. The least student unrest has occurred on the lowest-cost campuses — public community colleges and state colleges.) So the argument goes. Indeed, one hears the same arguments on the question of student charges that were raised initially in the nineteenth century about elementary schools, then secondary schools. If historical precedent holds true, tuition charges will, over the long run, continue to be a relatively small item on the current-revenue side of the state college budgets.

RELATIONSHIP BETWEEN SIZE AND COST The question of financing higher education is very much tied to institutional size. College administrators have not been averse to enrollment growth because higher enrollments do mean economies of scale, visibility within the state, and because of the distribution of state funds on the basis of student enrollments, larger appropriations. Yet there is just no doubt that all higher education will have to pay more attention to the influence of size upon students, faculty, programs, and institutional cohesiveness. Many of the largest public universities have developed various cluster-college arrangements in order to make the institutions manageable, and indeed some state colleges and regional universities have begun to move in the same direction. Western Washington State College has done just this by creating a college within a college.

The average enrollment in state colleges and regional universities was pushing 5,000 in 1967; by 1975 the average will be close to 10,000, unless new institutions are developed — a step, I think, far preferable to doubling the size of existing colleges. Still, there are no magic numbers that have yet been discovered that define the optimum size of a college for maximum efficiency consistent with attainment of educational objectives. This relatively simple question just has no simple answer, yet it is a question on everyone's mind. The experience within the California state colleges is that unit costs increase substantially until an enrollment of from 4,000 to 5,000 full-time equivalent (FTE) students is reached. After that, unit costs pretty much level off, even in a large institution with 17,000 students. If and when unit costs go up again is simply not known in California.

Arthur D. Browne in Illinois thinks that the optimum size of an institution in terms of unit cost is somewhere between 12,000 and 15,000 students. He has made the empirical observation:

When institutions expand beyond that figure, they usually strive to become comprehensive universities with extensive doctoral programs and research units. Beyond this point, the university changes its complexion. Divisions become professional schools or colleges. Separate libraries break out among these professional schools instead of housing all volumes under one roof. Public service and extension activities escalate. The more expensive habits of the more prestigious universities are required. . . . The moral: you must commence new institutions to siphon off enrollments when existing institutions reach 12,000 students or else you have another large, comprehensive, highly competitive university on your hands which competes with the "dominant" or established university for supremacy on the academic totem pole.

The Illinois and Ohio experiences are basically the same as California's when it comes to minimum enrollments for efficient operation. In Ohio it has been found that a minimum enrollment of 5,000 FTE students is necessary in order to operate a four-year undergraduate instructional program on an economical basis. A statewide committee looking at this problem in Illinois concluded that any new four-year college should have a minimum of 2,500 FTE students within four years and 5,000 students at the end of eight years. John Millett, chancellor of the Ohio system, applies a rule of thumb as follows: If instructional overhead (student personnel services, general expense, plant operation and administration) is as high as 40 percent of the operating budget, the institution is too small for efficient operation. But the real problem these days seems to be determination of maximum size, which the Illinois study committee equates with optimum size.

In any case, it would seem that all these questions relating to size should stand high among the priorities for state colleges. Modern methods of analysis and planning surely could be of assistance. It is difficult to think that the Pentagon's planning problems are more complicated than those of the state colleges.

One of the stumbling blocks to better planning in higher education, I suspect, goes back to what has been mentioned earlier, namely, a shortage of first-rate administrators who have the time to work on these problems. They are so beset with the immediate tasks of keeping the ship afloat that often they cannot find time for charting the course ahead.

Good secretaries, however, never seem to be upset by the press of numbers. I entered the president's office of a very large institution, and somehow his secretary confused my name with that of the person I was looking for. She didn't bat an eye and told me to wait; she had no doubt that there might well be someone with my name on the administrative staff she had not yet heard of.

5. One End of the Log— Students

In the fall of 1967, state college and regional university enrollment was 1,468,891, or 21 percent of all students in American higher education. Nationwide, 60 percent of the students are men and 40 percent are women; in state colleges, the figures are 53 percent and 47 percent, reflecting the strong feminine traditions of the institutions. But these aggregate statistics don't say very much about who these students are, where they come from, what they look like, how they dress, what their ambitions in life are. In a word, they are the sons and daughters of the "forgotten Americans," the phrase coined by President Nixon in his 1968 campaign to describe the millions of Americans who elected him President, people whose way of life is summed up by a term that is a pejorative in liberal intellectual circles but which still reflects much of what the nation is all about: middle-class values. These people are not black, poor, rich, or in the headlines.

TRADITIONAL STUDENT CULTURE The weather was warm and sunny when I visited the University of Northern Iowa in Cedar Falls. Students were making full use of the benches, grass, and tennis courts—as well as the courtyards of the dormitories, where girls sunned themselves in bikinis. I was struck at the very neat and orderly dress and manner of both the men and the women. There was not a real uniform, though chino pants and levis were common with the boys, and skirts, slacks, and shorts seemed to be evenly distributed among the girls. Compared with scenes in the East, girls' skirts seemed long and the hair short; but the contrast was greater for the boys. In two days I saw only one really long-haired fellow, though I am told there are many around. The atmosphere of the campus was uniformly pleasant and devoid of tension. Students laughed and chatted easily as they strode to and from class; there seemed to be little pressure hanging over the place. Moreover, students invariably smiled and said hello as I passed.

It was the week of the Spring Fling. On Monday there was the Miss UNI beauty pageant; on Tuesday, elections for "Your Favorite Prof" and "Favorite Man on Campus", on Wednesday, a hootenanny and beard contest. On Thursday, I attended the sack supper, Olympic games, and a civil rights rally. On Saturday there was scheduled a Mint Julep formal dance. The notices for these activities were posted all over the bulletin boards, giving a rather bacchanalian springlike air to the whole place, a common occurrence at this time of the year. But also on the bulletin boards were notices for a film series involving Pinter, Chekhov, and Giraudoux and a confrontation on the subject "What Is the Future of Martin Luther King's Dream?"

Ninety-eight percent of the students at Northern Iowa are Iowans. One-third come from very rural areas, one-third from more heavily populated counties, and one-third from towns with populations over 8,000. Most of the students see teaching as a step up the socioeconomic ladder. This is a very poor place for a girl to catch a rich husband. One-third of the students are from families with less than $5,000 a year income, a fact which results in UNI having more state scholarship funds than the two major universities combined. The majority of students come to UNI for vocational reasons. They tend not to be intellectual or bohemian in their orientation — they are there to get a teaching credential, which means a job.

UNI has been very much of a "suitcase college." Students automatically have taken off on weekends, not necessarily for lack of anything better to do around the campus. Many simply like it better at home. Activities do seem to be picking up each year, with more going on. One problem is how to involve the 35 percent of the students who are commuters and who are pretty much left out of campus activities. When asked about the shift to university status, one student said this was great because the national fraternities don't want to do business with colleges but now are interested because of their new university status!

Student leaders I met were rather discouraged by the general apathy of the students toward any kind of political activism or strong commitment toward the racial and urban problems at home or the Vietnam problems abroad; they wanted to do anything to stir up some kind of activity. They underlined the vocational spirit among most of the students. These elected officials said that most students think the student government is effective and that this is largely due to President Maucker, who takes a personal interest in it. I should note, of course, that radical students dismiss most student governments as company unions, part of the "system." The strong parietal rules and regulations, especially for the girls, were a big issue. In general, however, the student politicos seemed remarkably well satisfied with their role in government.

Visits to other campuses usually revealed carbon copies of what I have just described. East Carolina University is another suitcase college. Students all go to the beach on weekends, and the place looks like a ghost town. There is a curious mixture of apathy, vocationalism, provincialism, and a party atmosphere. President Nixon won the *Time* straw vote. There are supposedly a few hippies around, but very few indeed. Whenever anything gets stirred up, the football players always clamp down. Students are just as conservative as the community.

The prevailing atmosphere at East Carolina seems to be one of peacefulness, relaxation, and divorce from the major problems of the outside world. The students themselves are well tanned, mostly blond, and "all-American" looking. The uniform for the girls is dresses, and their hair seems to be generally well groomed. The boys are equally decorous, though often without socks. I would say without hesitation that student dress on state college campuses is dramatically more conservative than on more prestigious university campuses. One reason, as I learned at Trenton State College from a charming coed, is that the students are required to be presentable when they visit public schools either for observation or for student teaching.

Beards, long hair, dirty clothes, micro-miniskirts, hippies, beatniks, beads, student power, SDS, black power, the New Left, sit-ins, demonstrations—these are words used to describe the current collegiate generation. They are misleading when applied to most students at well-known university colleges, where much of the militancy has been found; they are even more misleading when applied to higher education in general. The fact is that the majority of students in state colleges and universities are not radicals and would not dream of tearing up the president's office. With lower-middle-class backgrounds, they are much more determined to obtain a college degree as the key to job security. Many are first-generation collegians whose attendance at college, despite relatively low cost, means considerable financial sacrifice for their families; indeed, many work their way through college. (Advice to parents: If you want a good, safe place where traditional middle-class values are still the norm, a state college may be the place for your offspring.)

CHANGING STUDENT VALUES But the scene is changing rapidly. Everyone knows about the militancy and rioting at San Francisco State College and in some other California state colleges. Indeed, the potential for violence is perhaps greater in AASCU institutions than elsewhere. The tradition of paternalistic if not authoritarian administrations in many of these colleges provides one important, explosive ingredient. A second is the oil-and-water mix of lower-middle-class whites and militant black students. The natural antipathy of the blacks who want status and the whites who don't want to lose it could lead to worse violence than has yet been seen on college campuses. Militant blacks are much more likely to stir things up on state college campuses than white SDS types, and the trouble is likely to be between white and black students, not between students and administration. This is an important difference from so-called liberal campuses, where white students flock to the side of the blacks.

In many state colleges the values of the students are changing. Traditionally very provincial, with a constituency from rural and small-town backgrounds, state colleges are spreading their networks of recruitment ever wider to the cities and suburbs; and inevitably with the growing cosmopolitanism and sophistication comes restiveness among the students, especially those in social science and the humanities. Students in the applied programs — elementary teaching, engineering, business, nursing, home economics — are not nearly so likely to break out of the traditional mold or to challenge authority. The same is true of the faculty in these areas. This has been the case even at City College in New York, where the engineers struggled hard to keep their campus open and were not willing to support black and Puerto Rican student demands.

Chico State College in California provides an example of changing student values. One hundred miles north of Sacramento in the Central Valley, Chico is an attractive town, prospering with its agricultural base of rice and almonds. Extremely conservative politically, with a strong John Birch influence, the town would seem to be a natural location for a cozy, equally conservative state college. In the past, Chico State was a small, traditional, rustic college with lots of ivy. Now this applies only to its outward appearance, for things are changing. Enrollment is growing very rapidly—now upward of 7,600 undergraduates—with just as rapidly increasing numbers of faculty, many of them new Ph.D.'s from all over the country. Teacher education has definitely been given a backseat within the past couple of years, and the percentage of people preparing as teachers is probably no more than one-third. Programs are truly multipurpose—nursing, engineering, business, agriculture, to name a few. But the liberal arts emphasis is equally strong. I was much impressed with what I saw.

The student culture is intriguing. Chico has a reputation for being easy to get into and easy to stay in—and this is the reason for some of its appeal. Additionally, it is smaller and is considered warmer and less impersonal than some of the other state colleges. From a parent's point of view it is undoubtedly "safer" than the more radical metropolitan institutions. A result is that the majority of Chico students now come from all over the state, many of them from relatively affluent families and many of them suburban types from major metropolitan areas. Students say that they come to Chico to get away from "tar and cement." They want to get out into the hills and countryside and attend a college with ivy on the walls. This—a traditional college—looks good to parents.

Whereas suburban parents think that Chico is a safe place, away from the evils of the city, it turns out that the suburban youths bring with them all the vices of the metropolitan areas, including babes, booze, and drugs. The daughter of a prosperous suburbanite in San Francisco was sent to Chico complete with car, apartment, lots of good clothes, and cash to spend; she spends her time living with her boy friend and goes around in bare feet and dungarees. Metropolitan sophisticates see nothing unusual in this; it still causes raised eyebrows on state college campuses.

It turns out that a few years back, Chico was named as one of the best party schools in the country by *Playboy* magazine. Western Michigan also claims that distinction! This kind of reputation may seem to be out of character with what I have already described about predominantly teacher training institutions—the lower-middle-class students, vocationalism, provincialism, apathy. But this description is quite compatible with a party atmosphere. Many students attend a place like Chico, Western Michigan, or East Carolina University specifically to develop a skill that will land them a job but also to have a good time and lots of parties. (I admit that this ambience was very appealing as I sat outside the student union on a beautiful day about noontime in the midst of a bevy of attractive boys and girls who were sitting in the middle of the lawn around a rinkydink piano played by students who came and went. Roses were in bloom, the birds singing, the sun strong—California is really too much!)

A complete divorce is made between living and learning. What students study has little relationship to how they live or what they believe in. Many students, perhaps the majority in American higher education, still accept the irrelevance of college studies to their lives. They realize that what they study does not really affect them, and unlike students at some of the major university colleges, they accept this fact—they do not rebel against it. If you are having a good time, with lots of parties, and still are en route to job security and affluence, why fight it? I suspect that a real distinction between the minority activists on our college campuses and the majority of students is tied to this very point: the activists refuse to accept this divorce between living and learning, while the great majority of students not only accept the divorce but do not want to bring about a reconciliation. There is another, related difference which concerns an assessment of the quality of American life. The protesters see the colleges as institutions training them to become "productive" members of a society of which they are highly critical. Unlike the many students who accept American life basically as it is, the activists reject it, its values, and more directly the educational system which is part and parcel of it. I shall return to this point later.

I met with a group of liberal, activist students, most of them narrowly defeated in recent elections. They say the campus is divided fairly evenly among conservatives, liberals, and radicals and that the conservatives won because they were much better organized and because the liberals and radicals split the rest of the vote. These students agree that, in general, the campus still fits the image *Playboy* gave it—with emphasis on athletics, parties, sex, drinking, fraternities, and sororities. But they say that this is changing slowly, that some of the activists are gaining ground, and that the place is in a state of transition. The liberal do-gooders lost the vote, but they came very close.

I asked what the changes from the *Playboy* image were. To illustrate, they said that sex is now open and direct, much more so than before; it is not promiscuity. It involves honesty and integrity, say the students, as opposed to the babes-and-booze philosophy that the *Playboy* image suggests.

ATHLETIC TALENT At many state colleges, extracurricular activities are partly financed by the students themselves, in the form of compulsory activity fees, and the students determine the allocation of their own funds. Traditionally, intercollegiate athletics has been by far the biggest item on the budget, and the sports program has had little difficulty garnering a large share of the available funds. But more recently, there have been on several campuses serious debates among the students over the size of the budget for athletics in comparison with other kinds of activities. The very evening I visited Chico, 400 students held a session with the power group that controlled the associated student funds and tried to get money away from the athletic budget into other organizations.

As one would expect, the San Francisco State students went at this matter with style. A radical slate of student leaders campaigned and won easily on a platform that called for financial support through the compulsory $10 activity fee of political, community-involved, and ethnic organizations—the Black Student Union, Third World Liberation Front, etc. Funds for traditional activities were cut to the bone, including the usually heavily subsidized football program. Some money was eventually restored, but football remains in rough shape. The college position has basically been that the duly elected student officials have the right to allocate the funds as they see fit. The state attorney general's office takes a different view, perhaps because of the political power of activist students with a lot of money in their hands. The result as of early March, 1969, was that the funds of the Associated Students were in receivership until the courts decided what was legal and what wasn't.

In short, the balance of power among students is beginning to shift at many state colleges, and this shift away from traditional collegiate values will mean increasing conflict between the values of the new protest generation of students and the traditional college culture epitomized by the athletes. Often the bane of a college president's existence, the athletes now are considered allies, part of the "establishment."

Intercollegiate athletics is really big time on many state college campuses. San Diego State, with 30,000 students, has been national football champion three years in a row through 1968 — in the unheralded College Division! I ran into an all-American track man, an Olympic candidate, who was brought up from the South on an athletic scholarship to a relatively small Midwestern state college he had not heard of until approached by the track coach. Grambling College in Louisiana and Jackson State in Mississippi, both Negro institutions, probably have sent more players to pro football than any other university except Notre Dame. The most recent pro football draft took no fewer than 11 men from these two colleges. Strong athletic ties are being built in many states between the junior colleges, which serve as a staging area for athletic talent, and the state colleges, which pick up the athletes once they have proved themselves. Low tuition and the lack of rigorous academic admissions standards make these state colleges ripe for pressures leading to big-time athletics. The charge of exploitation of black athletes is not limited, of course, to state colleges, but it may be worth noting that Harry Edwards, the black sociologist who started the movement toward a black boycott of the 1968 Olympic games, was a professor at San Jose State College in California.

Presidents with whom I spoke take differing views about the athletic situation. Some are sanguine, and others are openly critical about current intercollegiate sports, particularly football. The headaches, financial and otherwise, lead a few to the private opinion that intercollegiate football should be abolished. Leo Jenkins at East Carolina University, on the other hand, not only endorses intercollegiate athletics but sees no substitute for winning, and athletic trophies are displayed behind his desk. When the University of North Carolina abolished the Dixie Classic, a prestigious basketball tournament, Jenkins established the East Carolina Classic to take its place. He has advocated special academic arrangements for basketball and football players during the season that would give "athletes an opportunity to pursue both their athletic and scholastic programs, doing justice to both." They would enroll in special self-study courses and would not be required to attend classes. Jenkins believes this proposal would take pressure off the players to cheat and pressure off the professors to give breaks to athletes.

ACADEMIC TALENT In regard to academic rather than football talent, let's take a look at the American Council on Education (ACE) 1968 national norms study of incoming freshmen (Appendix C). About 85 percent of the students at four-year public colleges had been in the top half of their high school graduating classes, a figure paralleling all four-year college freshmen but lower than public and private university figures. Almost 50 percent of the public college freshmen were in the top quarter of their high school class, 24 percent in the top tenth. In terms of grades, 56 percent had high school averages of B or better, in contrast to 73 percent at the private universities and 64 percent at the public universities. Nevertheless, if grades mean anything, the public four-year colleges are getting a slightly stronger student than the Protestant colleges, for example, where the figure is 54 percent, or the junior colleges, with 30 percent.

I should note that when inquiring about how bright the students are in state colleges, one immediately runs into the objection of some faculty and administrators that this is an irrelevant consideration. They tend to see the mission of state colleges as teaching institutions serving the needs of mass education. Others, largely younger Ph.D.'s, regard this matter as decidedly relevant to their ambitions for higher institutional status.

The Coordinating Council for Higher Education in California did a survey of admissions requirements of state colleges around the country. The first thing they found was that in California both the university and the state college systems have the highest entrance requirements for public institutions in the country. Next, they found that requirements for admission to state colleges are generally lower than those for admission to state universities. However, they did find that some states have the same requirements for both institutions. Some states require their resident students to have a C average for admission to state colleges, four states require students to have been in the upper half of the graduating class, one state requires a rank in the upper two-thirds, and two states will take anything higher than the bottom quarter. Thirteen states require students to have passed 16 Carnegie units in academic subjects, and eight states, 15 Carnegie units. Thirteen states require only graduation from high school for college admission.

FRESHMAN PROFILE: 1968 The 1968 ACE norms study shows that, aside from junior colleges, the public four-year colleges have the oldest freshmen—4.2 percent are age 20 or older, in comparison with 3.2 percent in the public universities. In the junior colleges, the figure is four times that. Regarding secondary school achievement outside the classroom—

president of the student organization, major part in a play, varsity letter in sports, editor of the paper, participation in National Science Foundation summer programs, recognition in the scholastic honor society or in the National Merit competition—in all but one of these and similar categories, there is a lower percentage of state college students than of all four-year college students. Yet it is significant that as many as 26 percent were in their high school honor societies and that 5 percent gained recognition in the National Merit competition.

With regard to probable major field of study and career occupation, it is not surprising to find education high on the list—42.2 percent of state college students indicated public school teaching as a career. Experience is that this percentage rises as students progress through college. As for the major influence on the decision to attend a particular college, 32 percent of the state college students list low cost as a major influence. It ranks third, in the eyes of students, behind parental influence and academic reputation of the college (a category students always check!). Only junior college students pay more attention to the matter of cost. This point underlines the importance of college cost as a factor with lower-income families.

Only 31 percent of four-year public college freshmen come from metropolitan areas—suburbs or central cities. The state college constituency continues to be from independent cities, towns, and rural areas. Interesting figures emerge when we look at family educational background, occupation, and income. Only 12 percent of the fathers of state college students hold a college degree, the lowest percentage for any of the categories of institutions except the two-year colleges. Of the fathers, 26 percent are either skilled or semiskilled workers; another 26 percent are in business, which in the other kinds of colleges is by far the primary occupation of the fathers. One finds the sons and daughters of very few professional people in state colleges. Estimated parental income tells the real story: 38 percent of the students report family incomes less than $8,000; indeed, 8 percent report incomes less than $4,000. These figures parallel the public two-year college figures and are in sharp contrast to the higher income reported in other kinds of institutions. As one might expect, a higher percentage of state college students than of other four-year college students say that personal savings or employment are a major source of financial support during the freshman year—28 percent. At the same time parental or family aid is lower than at other four-year colleges and universities.

It is not surprising that there were more questions on demonstrations and protest in the 1968 ACE report than a year earlier. Less than 4 percent of the four-year public college freshmen said that the chances were good that they would participate in a demonstration in the future, the lowest figure for all colleges except the two-year colleges. In 1967, 47 percent thought that colleges were too lax on student protest; in 1968, the figure rose to 54 percent, a trend that ran true for all higher education except, again, for the junior colleges, where protestors have been in general disfavor all along. The point is that, if freshmen are to be taken seriously, only a very small minority have any idea of protesting and a growing majority believe that colleges are too easy on student protestors. This is true for higher education in general but especially true for freshmen at the public two- and four-year colleges.

The freshmen were asked about various activities during the past year, presumably their senior year in high school. It turns out that a somewhat higher percentage said that they had engaged in protests in the past than said they were likely to do so in the future! At the four-year public colleges, 4 percent protested against the Vietnam War, 7 percent against racial discrimination, and a whopping 16 percent against school administration! The figures were roughly parallel for all freshmen.

Some other figures: Ninety percent of the state college freshmen agreed that students should have a hand in designing the curriculum, 25 percent felt that the college should control student behavior off the campus, and 59 percent felt that the college should regulate student publications. Only 16 percent felt marijuana should be legalized (29 percent in private universities). Finally, 42 percent felt that disadvantaged students should receive preferential treatment—a higher figure than for either public or private universities.

A MEASURE OF CAMPUS ATMOSPHERE The College and University Environment Scales developed by C. Robert Pace of UCLA provide additional insights into what is known as the "environmental press" at different kinds of institutions. His widely used questionnaire deals with campus atmosphere along five different dimensions. The first is a practicality scale, which reflects the degree of vocationalism but also other personal and social benefits, such as parties, fun. (Recall the Chico students described earlier.) On this scale, so-called teachers colleges and state colleges rank at the very top, with selective liberal arts colleges at the bottom. A community scale grades qualities of faculty and school friendliness, student togetherness, and questions of decorum and consideration. Here, teachers colleges and state colleges are somewhat in the middle, with denominational colleges scoring highest and engineering and scientific schools lowest. I would have expected higher scores in the state colleges.

A third scale has to do with awareness: national and international perspective as opposed to a provincial or parochial view, opinions about contemporary society, the arts, and other matters. Here, teachers colleges and state colleges rank very much toward the bottom, just higher than the engineering and scientific colleges. The selective liberal arts colleges are at the top of this scale. The apathy that student leaders complain about in state colleges shows up clearly in this particular measure.

The fourth scale is propriety: consideration, caution, conscientiousness, personal behavior, self-control, pranks and escapades. Denominational colleges score highest here, but as one might expect, teachers colleges are next, and a bit further down are state colleges. The final scale is scholarship, reflecting high standards, study, and challenge, for example. Teachers and state colleges are at the bottom here. At the top are the selective liberal arts colleges.

In some respects, the state college population more nearly resembles the community college student population than it does other four-year colleges and universities. Both kinds of institutions draw students pretty much from the same barrel, so that one would expect their entering freshmen to be somewhat alike. Beyond that, the fact is that upper-division enrollments in large numbers of state colleges consist increasingly of junior college transfer students. Again, this is an argument for closer ties between the national organizations of the two kinds of institutions — AASCU and AAJC.

6. The Other End—Faculty

State college faculties are restive. We have seen how they jealously look over the fence at the university, where generally higher salaries, better fringe benefits, lighter teaching loads, and greater opportunities for research prevail. We have seen as well how rifts occur within college faculties as institutions expand their programs beyond teacher education and as enrollments begin to bulge. The old guard education faculty loses its influence, and the same kinds of split between academics and educationists occur in the former teachers colleges as has been evident for years in the more established universities.

ALBANY: THE TENSIONS OF GROWTH Let's take another look at Albany to illustrate some of the issues. I have mentioned that the architecture of the place—the buildings, their scope and design, their aspiration—is magnificent. The architect was Edward Durrell Stone. The style might be called classical modern; everything has a strong vertical thrust, with hundreds of white poured-concrete columns and vaulted archways. The pristine, white appearance is striking. The central academic podium consists of 14 major buildings arranged in a square around a large open courtyard, beneath which will be major instructional spaces. The vaulted roofs, supported by 40-foot-high columns, enclose the entire complex, which is seven city blocks in length. Four residential quadrangles fit each of the corners. There are fountains, landscaping, and luxurious interior decor to match the architecture. Wall-to-wall carpeting runs throughout, including the dining halls and the residential quadrangles.

There are some complaints about acoustics and corridor space. But to me the only disquieting note came from a student who said it all somehow seemed funny. Perhaps he was referring to the disproportion between the magnificence of the buildings and what he felt were the pedestrian concerns of the students themselves. The place looks like a cross between the Parthenon and the Woodrow Wilson building by Yamasaki at Princeton—but all multiplied 15 times over. One would expect nothing but edifying and world-shattering truths to emanate from such magnificence.

But if the realities are disproportionate to the aspirations of the place, Albany is in a hurry to narrow the gap. The institution is striving even at the cost of internal dissension to become a top-flight research university. At present, Albany is somewhat schizo-phrenic and perhaps embarrassed about all the attention it receives. Its future will be interesting to watch. As with many of the places I visited, I came away from Albany with mixed emotions: impressed by what I had seen—the excitement and fervor of an upwardly mobile institution, lots of tension and problems but with a definite focus on future greatness—yet disturbed by a gnawing feeling that somehow this sharp break with the past tradition of teacher educa-tion may leave a void that will be difficult to fill. It recalled David Riesman's notion of the academic procession, the snakelike move-ment by which every institution tries to be a Harvard. But what has happened at Albany?

In 1962, Albany became one of the four university centers in the SUNY system. In terms of prestige, it may still be at the bottom of the list; in terms of change, that can hardly be the case. In eight years the enrollment has more than tripled to the present 10,000 plus. There are now 950 faculty, 75 percent of whom arrived on the scene during the past eight years; 50 percent have been there no more than three years. There is much greater growth at the graduate than at the undergraduate level. Faculty say that the beautiful 400,000-volume library is in need of vast expansion to service the aspirations of the departments.

One reason for the choice of Albany as a university center was, as I mentioned, the fact that historically it had prepared secondary teachers and, therefore, had majors in the academic fields in con-trast to the other teachers colleges, which concentrated upon ele-mentary education. It was felt that it would be easier to develop a full-fledged university in an institution with such an academic base than it would be elsewhere, or than it would be to start from scratch. This assumption is debatable, judging from the experience at Albany.

The blunt fact is that the kind of work that goes on in an academic department within a major university is different from what goes on in the corresponding department even within a fine college with an excellent reputation. With good reason, the Vassar faculty in 1968 shied away from the move to Yale; as good an institution as Vassar is, many of its faculty felt insecure when contemplating how their relationships with the Yale faculty would be worked out. And working out faculty relationships is a vital matter when an institution takes on a new purpose and a new role. Many of the teachers colleges which have become new state colleges and, in turn, many of the state colleges now calling themselves universities have not had to face this difficult issue simply because they have changed the name without really changing the game. Albany not only changed its name, it very much changed its game.

The creation of 19 Ph.D. programs in just a few years has been no easy task. It has meant strenuous recruiting of top academic people for departmental chairmen, promising them strong financial support and facilities as well as a free hand in developing their departments for the kind of research and graduate work typifying that of major research universities.

Robert Allen, a top biologist at Princeton, was lured away to Albany both by a generous salary boost and by the promise of what could be developed there. He was made chairman of the biology department, which was housed in the largest academic building on the campus. His facilities are much better than what he had at Princeton, and money was initially easier to come by. In just two years, federal agencies had committed $2 million in grants to him and 14 new faculty members. He had inherited about 17 members of the old biology department, all of whom he likes, though a few are not real researchers. He made it quite clear to these people that in the future they would be judged on their scholarly publications as well as their teaching. In general, he has been delighted at how well they have responded to the new role; the two or three who are simply not interested are content with other responsibilities. In short, Allen is revolutionizing the biology department to make it a full-fledged research operation at the graduate level. He feels his department can stand alongside most in the country and is superior to those in many prestigious universities. Five fields are already pretty well established: developmental biology, cellular biology, ecology, biochemistry, and biophysics.

Allen was clearly hired as a star and has performed. He stands as something of a symbol of what the university hopes to accomplish—but I must add that he knows relatively little about public schools and the preparation of schoolteachers. His emphasis is upon his discipline, pushing back the frontiers of knowledge, and training graduate students. What has happened in biology is an Albany success story. Because Allen is a warm and decent man with a concern about people, he has been judicious in handling the merger of the old and new biologists.

In a few other departments this transition has not been as graceful. In one, faculty members with whom I spoke referred to the "blood bath" between the old and the new, the soft and the hard. One of the well-known men in the field came in as chairman, a superstar who brought with him enough new men to give him the balance of power within the department. Apparently, he then simply told the old guard to do research or get out. He took them off committee assignments, doubled them up in offices although many of them had been senior members of the department, and gave them lower-division teaching assignments although many of them had been teaching at the graduate level. The displaced older chairman had an outstanding reputation throughout the state in public school circles and had been a source of inspiration for countless hundreds of secondary school teachers. Today, he is simply ignored; he is about to retire, and very few seem to care.

The result of moving quickly has been considerable tension in some of the larger departments, where members of the old guard try to justify their inability to adjust to the new demands by falling back on arguments for protecting the teaching function. Departments like biology and romance languages have adjusted superbly and have top reputations. The English and history departments have not moved as rapidly; the new breed is still very much a minority because of the preponderance of senior faculty from the old days. One top administrator stated quite boldly that the criterion for hiring and promotion is scholarly competence, not teaching skill. Many of the old guard do exhibit a good deal of anxiety over promotion and tenure as a result.

But it is not simply the confrontation between the pre- and post-university faculty which causes problems. Development at Albany has meant a process of continually expanding expectations. Faculty hired between 1962 and 1964 considered themselves the bright new breed. Soon, an even newer breed arrived on the scene, and the earlier group then found itself in disagreement and difficulty with the more recent arrivals. It may be that those departments which began to grow the earliest also have the slowest rates of development as a result of this kind of increasing expectation.

Perhaps some of these problems suggest a contrary line of development to that taken by the SUNY system. It may well be that the most difficult place to transform into a university is the strong liberal arts college. Next in difficulty would come a place like Albany. Brockport, on the other hand, with its tradition of elementary education, might be easier since there would not be a large, established group of full professors in academic areas. Easiest of all, perhaps, would be to start a new institution.

Another result of trying to develop an existing institution is the impact on the budget. One faculty member at Albany made a comment about the waste of money in placating the old guard! The state was paying for first-rate performance from some second-rate people, in his opinion. Yet without such procedures the fabric of the institution would be torn apart; buying people off has its merits.

Having gone the furthest along the spectrum to full university status, Albany is surely atypical of state colleges and regional universities. Yet the faculty problem I have just described is one shared in varying degrees by departments in almost all these developing institutions. Debates rage over the question of teaching versus research, whether one can exist at a high level without the other.

Part of the confusion is over the definition of research and publication; there are many distinctions that can be made, none of them fully adequate. Traditionally, publications of faculty in teachers colleges, whether from professors of education or academic types, have had a very definite educational slant. Professors of mathematics have been mathematics educators, not mathematicians. Their publications have to do with advancing the teaching of mathematics, not with the advancement of mathematics as a discipline. In the shift to state college status and then to university status, the mathematics educator is expected to perform more as a mathematician and less as an educator. Elementary and secondary school textbooks are another form of publication that professors in teacher training institutions have long been noted for. But textbooks, whether for school or college, are simply not considered significant when it comes to publication review for promotion at a major university. Popularization of the discipline in highbrow magazines or newspaper reviews doesn't count for much either. What matters are books and journal articles which are written essentially to be read by colleagues within the discipline.

FACULTY AMBITIONS State college faculty members have been up in arms for several years about the unequal distribution of federal funds for research purposes. They want what they feel to be their share of federal largess and resent bitterly the vastly disproportionate amount going to the established universities. They have set up directors of research within their institutions, people whose job it is to help faculty members dream up research proposals, type them up, and see that they get submitted to the proper agency in Washington. There is an interesting reverse twist to this angling for research funds. Whereas the major universities must take pains to explain away the fact that about 50 percent of their annual budgets comes from the federal government, the state colleges play up for all their worth whatever funds they do receive. It is not that the large universities do not want federal support; they simply have some difficulty explaining to their alumni what it all means and often are in the posture of seeming to apologize for it. Not so with the state colleges, which equate each federal research dollar with one step upward on the academic ladder of respectability.

More state, federal, and foundation money, lighter teaching loads, research, doctoral programs, university status — these are all part and parcel of the same general package of faculty desire. Success and recognition in the academic world today are measured in research and publication acceptable to one's colleagues. In order to do the research, several things are necessary. There must be enough time, which means a university teaching load of something like 6 hours a week, in contrast to a typical state college teaching load of something like 12 hours a week. It means doctoral programs because doctoral candidates in the form of research assistants are invaluable aides in doing the research that leads to publication. In turn, a large input of money is necessary, often to purchase special equipment and supplies in the sciences, to provide financial support for the graduate student working on the project, and to subsidize books and journal articles. (I might add that the curtailment of research funds from the government in 1968 is not nearly so harmful in causing specific research to be left undone as it is in shutting off the financial support necessary for the continued supply of first-rate graduate students who will be doing the research of the future. For faculty research purposes, hiring professional, nonstudent assistants might make considerable sense in the absence of doctoral students. This scheme would surely be cheaper than mounting doctoral programs.)

Next, the argument goes, one cannot have access to sufficient money unless the institution has a name to attract money—hence the rush toward university status. A teachers college is less likely to attract federal or foundation money than a state college, which in turn does not have the attraction that the university holds for outside money. One last ingredient, of course, is the reputation of the department itself, which is determined by the quality of the staff. Staff quality results from the efficacy of the recruiting efforts, the success of which is determined by many things, including university status. And so the circular process continues.

Iowa State Teachers College became State College of Iowa in 1961. In 1967, it became the University of Northern Iowa. A minority of the faculty felt that changing the name of the institution in 1967 was not good without other changes, but the faculty voted 8 to 1 to proceed with the name change. Better educational service to the state of Iowa was a stated goal. But the arguments for the change were basically two: it would bring additional financial support, and it would make faculty recruitment easier.

There are many who question whether a wise move was made, especially since there are few signs as yet of additional financial resources. The graduate field is restricted to the master's degree in both education and liberal arts fields and to a specialist, sixth-year program. Interestingly, there is little or no pressure at the present time from any department for a doctoral program. With one exception, the faculty with whom I spoke were unanimous in saying that there were no researchers at Northern Iowa and that the place could not be considered a university. President Maucker described the institution as a university of medium scope. Many, including President Maucker, readily admit that it will take many years before the institution achieves full-fledged university status. Seven to ten years was seen as the amount of time needed to develop Ph.D. programs. One faculty member was outspokenly critical of the decision to become a university: not only was there no increase in funds from outside sources or from the state, but faculty recruitment was not made easier. This particular faculty member felt that while the first few institutions to assume the name *university* were able to get some mileage from it, now everyone is awake to the fact that names don't mean much; therefore, the dreams of money as lures to able faculty will not become realities.

An interesting phenomenon has occurred at Northern Iowa with respect to faculty recruitment, which continues to be a major problem. In the search for faculty members, they are getting fewer doctorates but better M.A.'s and near-doctorates. The percentage of faculty with doctorates at Northern Iowa, now about 35 percent, has been going down. At the same time, the general consensus is that quality is up. The very drive to get academically trained people from outside the usual teacher education orbit, with more emphasis upon recruitment from prestigious graduate schools, may make the institution look weaker when it comes to counting up doctorates. All the state college people with whom I spoke reject the thesis that soon there will be an abundance of Ph.D.'s, indeed a surfeit. Actually, they say, recruiting Ph.D.'s seems to get harder every year.

Patterns of recruiting have apparently changed greatly over the past few years in most of the state colleges because of the need to look more extensively as they seek out the new breed. Catalogs of many state colleges reveal a great deal of past inbreeding—faculty members with undergraduate degrees or master's degrees, sometimes both, from the institution at which they are teaching. Most of the faculty at a place like the University of Northern Iowa have taught in public schools, and most have been recruited from relatively nearby Midwestern universities. Their undergraduate work, if not their graduate work, has involved teacher education. When I suggested that this was the case to a professor of business administration at the University of Northern Iowa, he was puzzled because his department is moving away rapidly from teacher education. This particular man had been on the staff for just two years and had, in fact, not been prepared as a teacher. President Maucker says that as much as 80 percent of the faculty may have been through teacher education programs and that probably 20 percent have done their undergraduate or graduate work at Northern Iowa. But there are signs of change as efforts are made at Northern Iowa, as at other state colleges and regional universities, to bring in the kind of faculty who are wedded to their discipline, research, graduate students, doctoral work, and university status.

The source of these people is the traditional graduate schools, where, needless to say, the prices for their services inflate as departmental recruiters from across the country compete in the bidding.

The result is, of course, that the relatively poor state colleges lose out with many of the top prospects. Many of the young men and women recruited by state colleges are A.B.D.'s (all but dissertation). But the state college departmental chairman wanting to strengthen his department prefers an A.B.D. from a distinguished graduate department to an Ed.D. or to someone from a department in a second- or third-line graduate school. Thus the drop in the percentage of doctorates at a place like Northern Iowa.

More of these academic types, with or without Ph.D.'s, are desired by the departments to provide the upper-division majors and graduate work at the master's level. Yet it is the need for teachers in the lower-division, general education courses that brings forth funds from the state legislature. Money is made available to hire professors of English, for example, to take care of freshmen and sophomores, whose numbers are increasing. The professors of English being hired can't wait to gain position and rank so they may concentrate on what they have been trained for—research at the graduate level. Many of these people, hired to teach undergraduates, immediately want to turn this essentially teaching institution into a carbon copy of the research institution which they just left as graduate students. The situation is ironic, to say the least.

Reorganization of the institutional structure is tied to enrollment growth and to the gradual movement toward specialization, indeed professionalization, of the departments. The University of Northern Iowa is just in the process of moving into a university structure, with the usual series of university vice-presidents and deans and several colleges instead of just one. The current 15 departments, it is estimated, will become about 30. At present, the single department of language, literature, and speech, with 50 staff members, covers such diverse fields as religion, English, philosophy, speech (general, theater, and corrective), and foreign language; this department will be broken up into several. Education and psychology, now one department, will become two; the science department will become three; the social science department about three or four—and on it goes.

GOVERNANCE: SENATES, COLLECTIVE BARGAINING, UNIONIZATION Though I found that students in general seemed to be satisfied with their role in the governance of the colleges I visited, this was hardly the case with the faculty. I mentioned that faculty members seemed restive about their role vis-à-vis both internal and external governance. The further the institution moves along the spectrum toward university status, the more restive the faculty and the more concerned they are about their role in policy determination. Faculty senates are coming in everywhere, and as they do, the benevolent despotism of the president becomes more benevolent and less despotic. One faculty member I can recall in particular was very amusing in describing the situation at his institution. He was adamant about the fact that the faculty lacked a role in policy determination, but then he went on to say that the president of his institution is so benevolent a despot that the evils of the system are not really bothersome! He pointed out, for example, that he didn't have final authority even in choosing texts for his own classes; they have to be approved by the vice-president or a dean (or, more likely, a secretary who stamps the approval). But he had to admit that his requests are always granted. Even so, this faculty member sees in this practice a threat to academic freedom.

This kind of issue, coupled with second-class status alongside the university and with bread-and-butter disputes over salaries, teaching loads, and fringe benefits, makes collective bargaining and unionization topics of considerable discussion on some campuses—especially in California, New York, Michigan, and New Jersey. The issues are complicated and difficult to sort out. The first obvious point to make is that this discussion on some campuses in some states is part of the much larger effort on all state college campuses to increase the voice of faculty members in governance. Also, it is important to remember that in higher education, unlike industry, collective bargaining is not synonymous with unionization. Twenty-one states now have laws making it possible for public employees to organize for the purpose of collective bargaining through a single bargaining agent, but this does not mean that state college professors immediately join the American Federation of Teachers once they have decided to go down the collective negotiation road. Any one of a number of negotiating agents may be named, including faculty senates, independent faculty organizations, or local chapters of the American Association of University Professors or of the National Education Association. And even in these 21 states there remains the choice *not* to pick a bargaining agent. Rhode Island College, for instance, voted against collective negotiations through an exclusive agent.

The future is very difficult to predict. While collective bargaining is here to stay, it is not inevitable that unionization will sweep the state college campuses. Moreover, the experience with collective bargaining in higher education is so limited (about 25 faculties are involved) that the arguments pro and con are not easy to evaluate. The AFT takes a very dim view of the efficacy of faculty senates as an adequate voice for faculty participation and sees, of course, unionization as the answer. On the other hand, the AAUP rides two horses. One is the tradition of shared responsibility between administrators and faculty; but where, in fact, an adversary role does exist between the two, the AAUP backs collective bargaining, though not the AFT as the agent. Alfred Sumberg of the AAUP does not see collective bargaining as the real issue, rather how the process works and what the results are. In his view, much of the present negotiating is fruitless. Concentration on work rules can do much to impede educational innovation just at a time when innovation is sorely needed. Four basic areas of negotiation are the economic concerns of the faculty, a structure providing participation of members, guarantees of academic freedom and tenure, and grievance procedures. Sumberg does not think that the contracts he has seen deal adequately with these central questions. The AFT stresses the economic side. Meanwhile, the National Education Association is moving into higher education with the creation of a fairly militant group of three different organizations under the umbrella of what is called the National Higher Education Association (NHEA). The American Association for Higher Education (AAHE), the traditional higher education department within the NEA, is now a separate organization opposed to the adversary relationship between faculty and administration assumed by the new NHEA.

It seems to me that the basic point every faculty member must decide for himself is whether he looks upon his college administrators as colleagues or employers. Collective bargaining does assume the employer-employee adversary relationship of the industrial world. I sensed this atmosphere in a couple of the colleges I visited but noted, on the other hand, a collegial relationship in most places. Not that there were no grievances; rather that administrators were, after all, faculty members and everyone could work together. Ironically, when there is collective bargaining, the administrators are often caught in limbo and the negotiating is done by trustees and lawyers, who know least about the intricacies of college operations. This may help account for disappointment with the results.

From what I could see, younger and relatively insecure faculty members often take the lead in promoting unionization. That was my impression in California, and it is borne out in New York City. There, the City University of New York held a nationally significant jurisdictional election in December of 1968. The issue was not collective bargaining but determination of the bargaining agent under the Taylor Law. This was a jurisdictional dispute between the militant union and the more traditional faculty group. The older, tenured professors in a fairly close vote rejected the United Federation of College Teachers, a local of the AFT. The younger,

TABLE 19 *Estimated number of professional employees by employment status and primary function: state colleges and universities, fall term, 1966*

| Primary function | Full-time | | | | | | |
	Number	Percent	Total U.S., percent	U.S. public, percent	Percent of Total U.S.	U.S. public	Number
Resident instruction and departmental research							
Senior staff	52,179	78.0	63.6	62.6	18.6	30.5	7,750
Junior staff	1,308	2.0	3.9	3.8	7.6	12.5	6,646
Organized research							
Senior staff	354	0.5	5.9	6.0	1.4	2.2	162
Junior staff	129	0.2	1.9	1.8	1.5	2.6	167
Library							
Professional librarians	1,743	2.6	2.2	2.0	18.0	31.5	59
Other professional personnel	831	1.2	1.3	1.3	14.8	24.4	94
Extension and public service							
Formal instruction	653	1.0	1.9	2.7	7.6	8.8	1,592
Consultation	153	0.2	1.4	2.2	2.5	2.6	63
Other	126	0.2	1.0	1.4	2.8	3.2	20
Auxiliary enterprises	1,634	2.5	3.5	2.7	10.6	22.1	264
Schools operated by institution							
Elementary	1,570	2.3	0.5	0.7	64.8	81.4	89
Secondary	529	0.8	0.5	0.5	25.7	39.3	57
Other professional employees	5,692	8.5	12.4	12.3	10.4	17.0	268
TOTAL	66,901	100.0	100.0	100.0	15.2	24.5	17,231

SOURCE: Compiled by Carnegie Commission on Higher Education from U.S. Office of Education data.

part-time, and nontenured teachers (many of them moonlighting public school teachers who were already union members) voted overwhelmingly for the union. The result is two bargaining agents. The university's 4,500 tenured faculty will be legally represented by the Legislative Conference, the traditional faculty group within the university, while the 6,000 part-time and nontenured faculty members will be represented by the United Federation of College Teachers. This is the largest group of unionized college teachers in the country; their power, according to one observer, has made the Legislative Conference more militant. New contracts are said

	Part-time					Total full-time equivalent					
				Percent of						Percent of	
Percent	Total US., percent	U.S. public, percent	Total U.S.	U.S. public	Number	Percent	Total U.S., percent	U.S. public, percent	Total U.S.	U.S. public
45.0	40.0	31.1	9.3	19.2	56,090	75.7	59.5	57.3	18.1	30.3
38.6	32.0	34.3	9.9	14.9	3,594	4.8	8.5	8.8	8.1	12.6
1.0	2.1	2.5	3.7	5.0	426	0.6	5.4	5.5	1.5	2.4
1.0	9.4	13.0	0.8	1.0	198	0.3	3.4	4.0	1.1	1.5
0.3	0.5	0.4	5.9	12.1	1,763	2.4	1.9	1.8	17.5	30.5
0.5	0.3	0.1	16.9	47.0	866	1.2	1.1	1.1	14.8	24.8
9.2	10.1	12.5	7.5	9.8	1,100	1.5	2.9	3.8	7.4	9.0
0.4	0.6	0.8	5.2	5.8	166	0.2	1.3	2.0	2.5	2.6
0.1	0.5	0.6	1.9	2.5	134	0.2	0.9	1.3	2.7	3.2
1.5	0.9	0.7	14.3	27.9	1,827	2.5	3.1	2.4	11.3	23.6
0.5	0.2	0.2	23.1	40.3	1,605	2.1	0.5	0.6	62.5	80.0
0.3	0.3	0.2	9.4	20.4	549	0.7	0.5	0.5	23.9	38.2
1.6	3.1	3.6	4.1	5.7	5,801	7.8	11.0	10.9	10.1	16.5
100.0	100.0	100.0	8.2	13.3	74,129	100.0	100.0	100.0	14.3	23.0

TABLE 20 *Estimated number of full-time and part-time faculty in state colleges and universities by major area of teaching and/or research, fall term, 1966*

	Professors		Associate professors		Assistant professors	
	Full-time	Part-time	Full-time	Part-time	Full-time	Part-time
Agriculture and related fields	117	10	109	1	131	6
Architecture	9		9	1	17	3
Biological sciences	684	27	673	15	997	62
Business and commerce	630	23	653	55	1,277	209
Education and related fields	1,829	92	1,936	121	2,403	277
Engineering	216	13	298	38	425	78
English and journalism	970	31	1,016	20	1,809	122
Fine and applied arts	1,109	47	1,436	61	2,291	235
Foreign languages and literature	309	14	328	4	688	49
Forestry	6	1	15		12	
Geography	160	5	176	6	261	15
Health professions	119	8	182	27	451	56
Home economics	129		176	6	320	29
Law	32	13	27	5	20	20
Library science	34	1	76	6	151	24
Mathematics	382	5	577	22	1,133	87
Military science	34	2	32		194	4
Philosophy	130	3	125	5	213	19
Physical and health education	504	14	674	30	1,302	77
Physical sciences	781	27	914	22	1,298	60
Psychology	384	60	377	50	545	86
Religion and theology	7	1	13	2	19	2
Social sciences	1,284	173	1,286	73	2,297	200
Trade and industrial arts	66		92	7	172	23
All other fields	188	13	191	23	343	70
TOTAL	10,113	583	11,391	600	18,769	1,813
Percent of total U.S.	15	9	19	10	22	17

SOURCE: Compiled by Carnegie Commission on Higher Education from U.S. Office of Education data.

Instructors		Junior staff		Other academic faculty		Total		Percent of total U.S.	
Full-time	Part-time	Full-time	Part-time	Full-time	Part-time	Full-time	Part-time	Full-time	Part-time
43	9	10	9	12	12	422	47	5	1
8	1			12	15	55	20	3	3
362	109	114	468	7	59	2,837	740	15	10
766	326	41	459	41	106	3,408	1,178	20	11
*1,124	253	144	449	114	158	7,550	1,350	33	16
100	71	18	75	17	10	1,074	285	6	3
2,154	358	81	573	39	123	6,069	1,227	21	12
1,626	367	97	497	58	97	6,617	1,304	25	11
656	141	26	104	29	50	2,036	362	12	5
4	2					37	3	4	1
205	34	20	61	1	6	823	127	39	14
251	71	32	39	8	15	1,043	216	4	1
170	31	9	49	3	8	807	123	24	8
9	9		3		5	88	55	3	4
159	19	13	22	5	5	438	77	29	13
778	132	34	316	42	58	2,946	620	18	8
66		22		23	14	371	20	14	10
57	37	2	31	8	1	535	96	11	7
1,142	109	93	332	24	24	3,739	586	28	20
436	152	106	540	33	79	3,568	880	13	6
120	89	15	187	9	22	1,450	494	18	10
10	9	1			7	50	21	1	1
1,138	261	53	475	48	90	6,106	1,272	18	10
317	86	7	26	6	49	660	191	11	6
99	50	18	64	42	119	881	339	13	7
11,800	2,726	956	4,779	581	1,132	53,610	11,633	16	8
16	7	5	7	3	4	17	8		

to give CUNY faculty members the highest salaries in the nation.

Knotty problems of governance are bound to come up with collective bargaining, especially with unionization. For example, it is not at all clear how the line should be drawn between the responsibilities of a faculty senate and those of whatever group is officially recognized as the bargaining agent. Indeed, CUNY had just created a faculty senate prior to the election described above. I was told that faculty senates in Michigan became impotent once other bargaining agents were named. The collective-bargaining law in New Jersey was passed over Governor Hughes' veto; he had been concerned about the emerging faculty senates in the six state colleges. Another interesting question arises as to who negotiates with the union in a matter like salaries. In California, would it be the local administration, the chancellor's office, the state board of trustees, or the legislature, which in fact decides salaries through the budgetary process? To complicate matters still further, California is *not* one of the 21 states which mandates collective bargaining if the faculties vote for it. No one would be legally responsible to negotiate at all! Finally, the new thrust of substantive student participation in governance adds still another complication. Perhaps the students will have their union, too! (The Teaching Assistants Association at the University of Wisconsin is, in fact, the legal bargaining agent for 1,800 graduate students.)

AASCU FACULTY PROFILE Let's look further at state college faculty members. Tables 19 to 21 provide data that compare AASCU professional employees with their colleagues elsewhere. In 1966, there were 74,129 full-time equivalent professional AASCU personnel (14.3 percent of all professional staff in higher education), 80 percent of whom concerned themselves primarily with instruction. In higher education as a whole, 68 percent of the staff were primarily teaching faculty—a further indication of the teaching emphasis in AASCU institutions, where there are not the large numbers of graduate assistants manning sections in heavily enrolled lower-division courses.

In 1966, there were 53,610 full-time faculty members and 11,633 part-time. By field, education has by far the largest contingent, with 7,550 full-time people; next, in order, are fine and applied arts (6,617), social sciences (6,106), and English and journalism (6,069). Then there is a big drop to physical and health education (3,739), physical science (3,568), and business (3,408). When it comes to degrees held, 37 percent of AASCU professional staff hold the doctorate, in comparison with 42 percent in all higher education.

Some additional figures are interesting. Remembering that state colleges enroll 21 percent of all students in higher education, we note that they have 17 percent of all full-time faculty members and 8 percent of all part-time faculty members. This means that, on the whole, AASCU institutions have a less favorable student-faculty ratio than the rest of American higher education. They also depend less on part-time faculty. With regard to individual disciplines, 33 percent of the full-time education faculty in the United States are in state colleges. These colleges also have 39 percent of the geography

TABLE 21 *Estimated number of full-time senior teaching and research personnel by highest degree held and rank: state colleges and universities, fall term, 1966*

Rank	*Total number*	*Bachelor's degree or lower*	*Selected first professional degrees*	*Master's degree*	*Doctor's degree*
Professor	9,706	87	22	995	8,602
Percent	100	1		10	89
Percent total U.S.	100	2	7	14	77
Associate professor	11,248	158	43	4,941	6,106
Percent	100	1	1	44	54
Percent total U.S.	100	3	6	33	58
Assistant professor	18,271	656	77	13,333	4,205
Percent	100	4		73	23
Percent total U.S.	100	5	6	50	39
Instructor	11,671	1,443	103	10,069	56
Percent	100	12	1	86	1
Percent total U.S.	100	20	5	70	5
Other or no rank	564	184	4	326	50
Percent	100	32	1	58	9
Percent total U.S.	100	22	7	55	16
Total senior teaching faculty	51,460	2,528	249	29,664	19,019
Percent	100	5		58	37
Percent U.S.	100	9	6	43	42
Percent U.S. public	100	9	4	46	41
Percent of total U.S.	17.3	9.7	1.4	23.0	15.3
Academic dean	772	1	1	70	700
Percent	100			9	91
Percent U.S.	100	1	6	22	71

SOURCE: Compiled by Carnegie Commission on Higher Education from U.S. Office of Education data.

faculty, 29 percent of the library science faculty, 28 percent of the physical education faculty, 25 percent of the fine and applied arts faculty, and 24 percent of the faculty in home economics. At the low end, they have only 6 percent of the engineering faculty and only 3 percent of the law faculty. The fact that 67 percent of the education faculty in the nation are found elsewhere than in the former teachers colleges is important to remember. Within AASCU colleges, the education faculty represents only 14 percent of the total faculty, in comparison with 12 percent for all higher education. The point is that, contrary to popular belief, the former teachers colleges are not staffed entirely by professors of education!

FACULTY SALARIES   What do faculty salaries look like in the state colleges? The first point to be made is that, generally speaking, the public institutions in recent years have been increasing salaries at a faster rate than the private institutions, but this statement has to be tempered by the fact that the public institutions had further to go and had for many years lagged behind the private institutions. When one looks at total compensation, which includes both salary and fringe benefits, the public colleges and emerging universities had a greater increase in 1967-68 than the private colleges at all faculty ranks. The second point is that in 1968-69 the average of all public college salaries plus benefits rose 7.2 percent, an impressive figure except for the fact that the consumer price index rose by 4.2 percent. This means a real gain of only 3 percent. A 4.2 percent increase in compensation was necessary to stand still. Inflation takes its toll.

AAUP figures (*Bulletin,* June, 1969) show that the average compensation for full professors went up 9 percent in 1968-69; for instructors, 6.7 percent. That the greatest increase would come at the full-professor level is significant because, generally speaking, the state colleges and regional universities are least competitive when it comes to attracting senior faculty. One definition of the emerging institutions is weakness at the upper ranks. They are able to hold their own reasonably well at the lower ranks.

Bearing in mind that total compensation includes fringe benefits, which are about 8 percent of the total, the average compensation in public colleges and emerging universities was as follows in 1968-69: professor, $16,539; associate professor, $13,193; assistant professor, $11,032; instructor, $8,691. The full professor's compensation runs about $2,000 below that of his counterpart at the major state universities and about $5,000 below the salary and fringe benefits of full professors at the major private universities, but he also receives $1,500 less than his counterpart at a junior college. He gets a C rating on the AAUP scale.

The gap narrows at the lower ranks. The average compensation for associate professors gets a B rating; for assistant professors and instructors, A. Even so, at these same lower ranks, the public junior colleges run somewhat ahead of the public colleges and emerging universities. This is of great importance because it means that the public junior colleges are highly competitive with the public four-year colleges when it comes to attracting faculty. An instructor at a public junior college with average compensation of $8,747 receives $500 more than an instructor at a major public university! (Junior colleges without academic ranks are not included in the figures.) Though it is certainly true that faculty compensation in public colleges and emerging universities is not way out of line with other kinds of institutions, it does appear to be true that their position needs improvement if they are to compete with major public and private universities on the one hand and with junior colleges on the other.

7. What Shall Be Taught?

The greater the aspirations of a place, the flashier the jacket design on its catalog. One test of the ambitions of a college is the number and attractiveness of the pamphlets, brochures, bulletins of information, and catalogs that are available. Established institutions do not have to attract the public eye; emerging institutions want to do just that. Such is my conclusion after perusing many state college catalogs in an effort to get to know their curricular offerings.

WHAT ISN'T TAUGHT Once past the jacket design, one is overwhelmed by the diversity of programs found in state colleges and regional universities. Before looking at what does exist, it is interesting to note what doesn't exist. One characteristic of the major, well-known universities is the presence of law and medical schools. None of the institutions I visited had either, and no more than a handful can be found in AASCU institutions. Generally speaking, the state university rather than its regional younger brother has cornered the market in law and medicine. The monopoly on these prestigious professional fields will not be surrendered easily by the major state universities for a number of reasons, including the political clout that alumni in these areas often provide. In many states, legislators are graduates of the university law school, an obviously important tie from the point of view of the university president.

Also noticeably missing from the programs of state colleges and universities is advanced work leading to doctoral degrees. Many institutions are still deeply involved in the process of developing full-fledged bachelor programs. Others are pushing hard on master's programs; only a few are seriously undertaking doctoral work. A sizable number have instituted an intermediate degree between master's and doctorate, often called a *specialist degree* and designed primarily for public school personnel in administrative and supervisory positions that require training beyond the master's but short of the doctorate. Many of these programs also purport to train junior college teachers. The education specialist degree (Ed.S.) is gaining in popularity; some would say that this degree is actually a foot in the door for the doctoral degree—but more of this later.

When it comes to doctoral degrees (Table 22), the numbers are slim indeed. Between 1960 and 1966 there were only 1,237 degrees awarded, representing just over 1 percent of the total number awarded in the nation. These doctorates came from only 16 institutions: North Carolina College at Durham (Negro) (1), Texas Women's University (54), Colorado State College (485), Lowell Technological Institute (8), University of Southern Mississippi (42), North College of Engineering (10), SUNY at Albany (14), East Texas State University (12), Northern Illinois University (11), Ball State University (30), Wichita State University (2), SUNY at Buffalo (363), Bowling Green State University (5), University of Akron (46), University of Toledo (14), North Texas State University (140). Sixty-nine percent of the total 1,237 doctorates were in education. These represent 16 percent of all doctorates in education granted between 1960 and 1966. For the entire nation, only 6 percent of all doctorates granted were in education, in contrast to the 69 percent in these institutions. A significant policy issue is whether these

TABLE 22 *Doctorates granted, baccalaureate holders earning doctorates, and Woodrow Wilson fellows of state colleges and universities by size of institution*

1967 total enrollment	Doctorates granted 1960-1966	Number of doctorates earned (1960-1966) by baccalaureate holders	Number of Woodrow Wilson fellows awarded (1945-1967)
Less than 1,000	0	55	0
(Number of institutions)	(0)	(9)	(0)
1,000-5,000	55	2,179	100
(Number of institutions)	(2)	(122)	(52)
5,000-10,000	571	3,530	239
(Number of institutions)	(6)	(77)	(45)
Over 10,000	611	2,654	166
(Number of institutions)	(8)	(28)	(27)
TOTAL	1,237	9,418	505
(Number of institutions)	(16)	(236)	(124)
Total U.S.	92,863	80,878	14,326
Percent of total U.S.	1.3	11.6	3.5

SOURCE: Compiled by Carnegie Commission on Higher Education from National Academy of Science, *Doctorate Recipients, etc.,* Washington, D.C., 1967, and Woodrow Wilson National Fellowship Foundation, *Woodrow Wilson Fellows 1945-1967,* Princeton, N.J.

emerging institutions should go into doctoral programs and, if so, in what areas. The state colleges in California, as we have seen, can enter into joint programs with the University of California. But this procedure is controversial there, and the question persists in these emerging institutions throughout the country.

BACHELOR'S AND MASTER'S PROGRAMS
At the undergraduate and master's levels, programs of all descriptions can be found. Let me use California as an example. The 18 state colleges offer over 700 bachelor's degree programs, as well as the 350 master's programs. And even the listing of these programs does not give the full story since there are many options and special emphases within particular programs. A bachelor's degree in business administration is likely to mean anywhere from five to ten different emphases.

In turn, the more than 1,000 degree programs can be divided into as many as 23 different major subject areas: agriculture, architecture, area studies, business, city and regional planning, creative arts, criminology, education, engineering, foreign languages, health sciences, home economics, humanities, industrial arts and technology, library science, mathematics, natural resources, nursing, physical education and recreation, psychology, sciences, social sciences, and special majors. Under agriculture there are no less than 30 different programs at Fresno, Chico, and Cal Poly at both Pomona and St. Luis Obispo—colleges serving primarily agricultural regions. One can take everything from fruit production and animal husbandry to something called international agriculture. Under area studies, Latin America is common.

City and regional planning programs are either new or anticipated in the near future at several colleges. Creative arts runs all the way from well-developed music programs at several of the colleges to a master's program in radio-television-film at San Francisco State. The full gamut of engineering programs can be found, especially at the two polytechnic colleges. French, German, and Spanish are the most frequently offered languages, though Russian appears to be not far behind. Humanities includes only two programs in the classics but a number of master's programs in linguistics. In natural resources, degrees are available in everything from forestry, fishery, and wildlife management to oceanography. No fewer than 12 kinds of biology programs can be found—from the life sciences through oil physics and microbiology. Every branch of the social sciences seems to be represented: anthropology, economics, geography, history, political science, government, international relations, public administration, public service, social welfare — and on the list goes.

TEACHER EDUCATION

In education there are actually very few degree programs in California colleges. The existing bachelor programs are being phased out. That there would be very few bachelor's degrees in education may come as a surprise to those unfamiliar with what has occurred in teacher education over the past few decades. Programs in teacher education have three components. The first is general education, which means exposure in one way or another to the traditional disciplines of language, literature, history, and the social and natural sciences. This program is usually concentrated in the first two years (and in most institutions in this country is the very same program for all students, regardless of their upper-division majors). In the last two years, a student preparing to be a secondary teacher of English, for example, majors in English just like the usual English major. His major constitutes his second element in a teacher preparation program. The third element is the so-called professional sequence consisting often of an introductory course in education, a course in either the history or philosophy of education, a course in educational psychology, and some kind of methods work, usually tied in with practice teaching. This professional sequence replaces the usual free electives.

The point is that, as far as secondary education is concerned, there is no such thing as an education major. A student majors in and is identified with a particular discipline. This accounts for the difficulty in identifying the number of teachers an institution prepares. The only education majors left are usually found in those institutions which train elementary teachers and where the traditional kind of program remains — that is, the potpourri of introductory courses in the several different areas taught by the multipurpose elementary teacher. However, in a number of states, including California, these institutions now require an academic major of elementary teachers and have eliminated bachelor's degrees in education.

I noted earlier that teacher preparation is big business in all American higher education. About one-third of all bachelor's degrees every year go to students prepared as teachers. Liberal arts colleges, in particular, have a heavy percentage of their students preparing as teachers.

Figures in 1966 show that the state colleges and universities prepared 47 percent of all those eligible for initial certification as teachers in the nation's schools. The fact that a set of institutions with only 21 percent of the nation's students still prepares 47 percent of the nation's teachers is surely a reflection of a continuing mission despite the expanding role of the state colleges and regional universities.

It does not appear to be the case that the supply of teachers is shrinking as institutions become multipurpose in nature. The percentage of graduating seniors prepared to teach does go down — now about 62 percent in state colleges — but in absolute numbers teacher production goes up because of vastly increasing enrollment. Whether this production will keep pace with the demands of the schools is another question and one that deserves a close look.

The general attitude of many college and state officials I ran across was one of lack of concern. One man in New York State spelled out an interesting point of view. He was appalled at the old normal school system, which shanghaied girls into elementary education. The purpose of the normal schools was clearly to meet manpower needs of the state at the elementary school level. The idea was to give girls "the cheapest, lousiest education you could get away with." In his view, New York State turned the corner in 1960 with an entirely new outlook about the purpose of publicly supported higher education. Everyone seems to agree that a change took place, but perhaps without realizing what it has been all about! Specifically, the notion has been to develop a variety of programs to serve students, not manpower needs of the state. Manpower problems in various areas of nursing, engineering, and education may be met, but only as a by-product of the goal to provide a variety of educational experiences that meet the desires of a diverse student population.

This view means that SUNY has no more of an obligation to turn out teachers for the public schools than it has an obligation to provide sufficient nurses or engineers. It is left to these fields themselves to compete for and attract people, implying that the way to maintain the supply of teachers, for example, is to make the teaching profession an attractive one. And that is someone else's business, not SUNY's. This view is becoming common in state after state, as the former state teachers colleges become multipurpose and come out from under the control of the state departments of education. In New Jersey, certainly, this fundamental conflict over the purpose of the institutions is at the heart of much of the controversy in higher education.

Traditional ties between the public schools and the former teachers colleges through a common state board have been largely broken; still the certification mechanism tends to promote apparent conformity in teacher education programs. James Conant concluded in his 1960 report on teacher education that despite the appearance of conformity, there was a great deal of disagreement about what the actual content of teacher education ought to be. The one point of general agreement was that the most significant element in the program is practice teaching. Conant recommended that the state should enter the picture at that point in order to ensure satisfactory practice teaching arrangements. Beyond that, his recommendation was that the colleges and the universities should have maximum freedom to develop whatever teacher education programs they wished on an all-institution basis but then have the corresponding responsibility to defend their product. In short, the Conant notion was to introduce a great deal more flexibility and innovation into teacher education.

In wandering about, I often asked if anything had come of the Conant recommendations. From what I saw, very few bold departures from current practice have emerged. The reason is as much the general conservatism of faculty as it is the reluctance of state officials to promote change. Over the past eight years there apparently has been attention paid to improving practice teaching and the associated methods work. More is being made of technology. On the whole, however, the picture seems not to have changed much. In several of these institutions there have been major changes—but not in education. Academic vice-presidents and deans were frank in expressing their concern about the lack of progress in education as compared with other departments and schools within the institution. Weber State College in Ogden, Utah, is an exception. The entire professional sequence is being scrapped, and an exciting new program is under development. The emphasis is upon behavioral outcomes, not courses, and upon the continuous progress of students toward these behavioral goals. There will be a great deal of programmed learning, independent study, use of media, and sensitivity training, as well as contact with schoolchildren. Moreover, in minimizing traditional lecture and classroom procedures, the program will in itself provide an instructional model for future schoolteachers.

When visiting college campuses, I asked the students to evaluate their programs. In regard to teacher education, there were many of the same complaints I had heard eight years ago—Mickey Mouse courses, irrelevant, repetitious, poorly taught. On the other hand, some of the most vigorous complaints had to do with the lower-division general education courses, about which the same things were said. Apparently, many of the state colleges have not caught up with improvements in secondary education and are teaching the same old stuff year after year. As for the upper-division majors, the students often complained that their courses in English, for example, were geared primarily to future English teachers, with constant reference to what might be of use in secondary school teaching.

A few students as well as faculty commented upon the lack of innovation and experimentation. There is apparently some use of television in state colleges and universities, and some places, like Brockport, are in the process of planning multimedia instructional centers which will be of use to faculty interested in something other than the traditional lecture hall and classroom. This scanty innovation in teaching is not surprising in view of the models these institutions have chosen — the prestigious universities, which are known for their remarkable resistance to change. SUNY's experimental state college at Old Westbury, Long Island, is worth watching as perhaps the most "way-out" state college in the country.

THE TRANSFER PROBLEM

To talk about the four-year curriculum in state colleges is interesting but misleading. The single fact is that many graduating seniors have attended two or more colleges. The rapid growth of community colleges across the country means increasing numbers of transfers. Large numbers of upper-division students will have had their lower-division work elsewhere.

The goal in the California master plan is to divert lower-division students to the state's junior colleges so that the resulting ratio of lower-division to upper-division students in the state colleges and universities is 2 to 3. The state colleges have practically achieved this now, though the university has not. Complicated formulas are used to fix the admissions standards to conform with this policy. Actually, there are many more freshman women at the state colleges than freshman men. The admissions criteria at the present time work against men because of their poorer secondary school records. The girls have better grades and rank higher, but they also take somewhat easier courses. Attrition is upwards of 50 percent for the first two years, especially with the women. Then male junior college transfers more than make up the difference, so that by the senior year there are more men than women.

The state colleges as a whole probably graduate as many junior college transfers as they do their own freshmen. The main flow of California students today is initially into the junior colleges, and the main flow from the junior colleges is into the state colleges — almost five times as many as into the university and almost eight times as many as into private colleges.

And as two-year college systems continue to multiply and as the number of students enrolled in two-year colleges expands rapidly, this process will hardly be unique to California.

Already, state colleges elsewhere are feeling the effects of transfer pressures from community colleges and are working out the sometimes complicated negotiations that may be necessary to ease the problems of transfer. And this is not just a matter of less able students being siphoned off to the community colleges as a test of their ability to handle college work. Again, in California, a substantial fraction of students eligible for immediate entry to the university and the state colleges choose instead to enroll at a local community college — often for financial reasons — before moving on to a state college. At both state colleges I visited in California, the student reaction to the transfer business was very positive indeed; the students at Chico with whom I spoke happened all to be junior college transfers who were quite happy with their experience both before and after transfer. At Cal State Los Angeles, a commuter college serving primarily low-income students, one of the leaders of the Mexican-American group stressed his belief that East Los Angeles City College, a two-year community college, provided better and more personal instruction at the lower-division level than did the state college, and, therefore, this was the place that he recommended for Mexican-Americans, many of them marginal students academically.

The flow of students in California as well as in other states raises an interesting question. In those states where community colleges are picking up an ever-increasing proportion of first-time freshmen, might it not make sense for the state colleges, as well as the state university, to give up the lower division entirely and to become upper-division and graduate institutions? Florida Atlantic University and the University of West Florida have done just that; they are upper-division institutions. Richmond College, a unit of the City University of New York, is likewise an upper-division college that enrolls students directly from expanding junior colleges within the city system.

This arrangement would seem to be a natural for a place like Cal State Los Angeles; indeed, this was an upper-division college until 1959. President John Greenlee would not be opposed to dropping the lower division for a number of reasons. The junior colleges do a good job, and the transfers do as well as the indigenous students. If the community colleges enrolled all lower-division students, the present brahmin system of de facto differentiation of institution by race and social class would be broken up. Many of the Cal State faculty, despite protests to the contrary, are not really interested in lower-division teaching, and the number of freshman applicants and admittees has declined each year. Graduate enrollment pressures, on the other hand, are very strong. There is the further point that it is difficult to see how an institution can be all things to all people; something inevitably gets shortchanged. Finally, the students at Cal State are commuters, so that the old arguments about school spirit and the sanctity of the residential four-year experience are suspect.

I hasten to add that most of the state college people with whom I have spoken argue vehemently against dropping the lower division. Their arguments are many. The major objection is that the junior colleges do not do a sufficiently good job of providing a base for the major. Others talk about the importance of four years in the same place; still others, about the necessity for proper faculty development in a four-year program. In California, an argument is that lower-division courses, with their much higher student-teacher ratios, enable state colleges to offer specialized upper-division work which they could not otherwise afford—an interesting argument but hardly one that supports the educational superiority of lower-division work in the state colleges! This may be the best argument for dropping the lower division.

It does not appear that many colleges and universities, public or private, have as yet faced up to the implications of the flow of transfers from the community colleges. It does strike me that the further along the spectrum of development the state colleges proceed, the more difficulty they have with providing first-rate general education programs for their lower-division students. In this respect, they resemble the larger and more established universities, which are notorious for their mishandling of lower-division students. And one wonders if some of the more frenetic institutions with heavy lower-division attrition and equally heavy transfer pressures, increasing emphasis on graduate work, and larger proportions of research-type faculty might not well consider severely restricting enrollments at the lower level, if not eliminating them entirely. The opportunity for collaboration and cooperation between the faculty of state colleges and that of community colleges would be great; indeed, cooperative arrangements must proceed in any case.

A question is always raised about how well transfers do when they move from junior to senior colleges. This is a crucial issue from the viewpoint of the four-year college. The evidence is not conclusive, according to an ACE study in 1965. Perhaps the major conclusion is that one cannot make judgments concerning the performance of transfers independent of the context of the colleges in which they enroll and of the state system in which these colleges are found. The ACE study revealed vast differences in the success of transfer students in 43 participating colleges and universities in 10 different states. A student's chance for success depends very much upon his choice of four-year college and his choice of department in relation to his previous academic record. One would expect just such a conclusion. Colleges differ markedly in their admissions standards, financial-aid arrangement, degree of curricular diversification, and sophistication of guidance and help for incoming students. ACE published in 1966 *Guidelines for Improving Articulation between Junior and Senior Colleges* to help maximize the likelihood of successful transfer. The role of the new College Level Examination Program (CLEP) of the College Entrance Examination Board remains to be determined; it could help considerably with the often knotty questions of equivalency and credit transfer.

In Indiana, there are problems of a different sort. The state university has effectively curtailed development of an autonomous community college system, and at the same time there is an open-door admissions policy to the public institutions. Any secondary school graduate can go to any one of the state campuses—Indiana University, Purdue, Indiana State University, or Ball State University— if he applies enough pressure on the admissions office. Ball State has worked out a special deferral program of admission for students who rank below the middle of their graduating classes and have SAT scores below 400. These students are brought in and advised in August of special reading they must do before they can be admitted in either the winter term or the following spring term. The weakest of these apparently get the message and don't apply at all, while the others seem to be well motivated and come to college prepared to work hard. Before this device was adopted, only about 10 percent of low-level students survived; now upwards of 30 percent survived.

Even so, the overall attrition is as high as 50 percent during the first two years. Victor Lawhead, dean of undergraduate studies, is very concerned about the 4,000 students who drop out by the end of the sophomore year and for whom Ball State really serves as a junior college in spite of the four-year design of the program. At present there is very little formal mechanism on the campus for dealing with the educational needs of these students for whom the bachelor's degree is an illusion.

There is a real danger here. State colleges and regional universities have traditionally been teaching institutions concerned about accepting students as they are and working with them. The large group of students now benefiting from this tradition will suffer as these institutions move along the spectrum toward multipurpose university status, focusing interest and money on the upper-division and graduate levels, with a resulting decline in the quality of the lower-division programs. I am not saying that these interests are all bad, rather that they do call for a new look at institutional purpose and structure.

CURRICULUM REFORM A new look is needed at the curriculum as well. On the whole, state college students are surely not "turned on" by what goes on in the classroom, especially in general education. We know that colleges, regardless of reputation, have little impact on student values. Is it possible to revamp the curriculum in such a way as to excite apathetic students, on the one hand, and to redirect the energies of the more militant activitists, on the other? Perhaps not, but let me suggest an approach to the problem.

Psychologist Kenneth Keniston at Yale has studied student unrest here and abroad and in a recent article (*New York Times Magazine,* April 27, 1969)[1] set forth an interesting analysis of what is taking place — an analysis that goes deeper than immediate issues of the war, racism, drugs, violence, and law and order on the campus. It gets at cause, not just symptoms.

In the first place, modern societies have extended the time of disengagement of young people from the workaday problems of everyday life. This extension of youth well into the twenties "provides opportunities for intellectual, emotional and moral development that were never afforded to any other large group in history." Society through its colleges creates its own critics, "an ever-larger group of young people who take the highest values of their society as their

[1] Copyright 1969 by The New York Times Company. Reprinted in part with permission.

own, who internalize these values and identify them with their own best selves, and who are willing to struggle to implement them. At the same time, the extension of youth has lessened the personal risks of dissent. These young people have been freed from the requirements of work, gainful employment and even marriage, which permits them to criticize their society from a protected position of disengagement." But why the especially harsh judgment of society today?

Keniston suggests that it has to do with the end of an old order and the beginning of a new one. We are in the process of transition from the end of the industrial revolution to the beginning of the postindustrial revolution. In the most advanced nations, men can now produce more than enough to meet their material needs.

The transition from industrial to post-industrial society brings with it a major shift in social emphases and values. Industrializing and industrial societies tend to be oriented toward solving the problems of production. An industrial ethic—sometimes Protestant, sometimes Socialist, sometimes Communist—tends to emphasize psychological qualities like self-discipline, delay of gratification, achievement orientation and a strong emphasis on economic success and productivity. The social, political, and economic institutions of these societies tend to be organized in a way that is consistent with the goal of increasing production. And industrial societies tend to apply relatively uniform standards, to reward achievement rather than status acquired by birth, to emphasize emotional neutrality ("coolness") and rationality in work and public life.

The emergence of post-industrial societies, however, means that growing numbers of the young are brought up in family environments where abundance, relative economic security, political freedom and affluence are simply facts of life, not goals to be striven for. To such people the psychological imperatives, social institutions and cultural values of the industrial ethic seem largely outdated and irrelevant to their own lives. . . . Today, the moral imperative and urgency behind production, acquisition, materialism and abundance has been lost.

Keniston goes on to argue that campus unrest represents a fusion of the two revolutions. Black militancy amounts to the last stage of the successful industrial revolution in the sense that this revolution has involved "the progressive extension to more and more people of economic, political and social rights, privileges and opportunities originally available only to the aristocracy, then to the middle class, and now in America to the relatively affluent white working class. It is, in many respects, a *quantitative* revolution. That is, it concerns itself less with the quality of life than with the amount of political freedom, the quantity and distribution of goods or the amount and level of unjustice." This is what the American dream has been largely about.

As the United States approaches the targets of the first revolution, on which this society was built, to be poor shifts from being an unfortunate fact of life to being an outrage. And, for the many who have never experienced poverty, discrimination, exploitation or oppression, even to *witness* the existence of these evils in the lives of others becomes intolerable. In our own time the impatience to complete the first revolution has grown apace, and we find less willingness to compromise, wait and forgive among the young, especially among those who now take the values of this old revolution for granted—seeing them not as goals, but as rights.

They become nonnegotiable demands.

But impatience to complete the old revolution is matched by a desire to get on with the new revolution, which is concerned with issues "less social, economic, or political than psychological, historical and cultural." The industrial revolution was quantitative; the new revolution has to do with the quality of life. Students are vague in defining what they have in mind, but some trends are clear. The first is an antipathy toward quantitative and materialistic ideas, instead, a stress on the "joyfulness and zestfulness of experience. There is a new sensory awareness: an 'expansion of consciousness'; the stress on the expressive, the aesthetic and the creative; the emphasis on imagination, direct perception and fantasy." Rationality is played down; the emotions are played up.

There is "a revolt against conformity, equalization, standardization and homogenization—not against technology itself, but against the 'technicalization of man'." Difference, diversity, uniqueness, and individualism are sought: everybody "does his thing." Keniston speaks of a "post-homogeneous America in which cultural diversity and conflict are underlined rather than denied."

The new revolution also involves a continuing struggle against psychological or institutional closure or rigidity in any form, even the rigidity of a definite adult role. Positively, it extolls the virtues of openness, motion, and continuing human development. What Robert J. Lifton has termed the protean style is clearly in evidence. There is emerging a concept of a lifetime of personal change, of an adulthood of continuing self-transformation, of an adaptability and an openness to the revolutionary modern world that will enable the individual to remain "with it"—psychologically youthful and on top of the present.

Participation is a key characteristic of the new order. It means involvement, whether in the governance of universities or in the educational process itself, where relevance means "a chance for the student to participate in his own educational experience in a way that involves all of his faculties, emotional and moral as well as intellectual." Participation or involvement, together with the emphasis on individuality and an openness to new experience, is related to a new ethic of human relationships in which "individuals confront each other without masks, pretense and games." In talking with students today, one is immediately struck by their lack of pretense, their disarming honesty and directness. It is both refreshing and disconcerting.

Keniston points out that the students themselves rarely make this distinction between the two revolutions. Issues of the first revolution (racism, imperialism, exploitation, war) get mixed with issues of the second (experiential education, new life styles, meaningful participation, etc.). This is important since, otherwise, there is a moral dilemma involved. Would it be right for affluent Americans to seek out what appear to be self-indulgent goals of postindustrialization when millions of people in the world live in poverty and deprivation? Or, put another way, there could be an obvious clash between black students who want a piece of the action from the old revolution and affluent whites who look down their noses at these concerns. But student unrest mixes the old and the new through an "urgent need to fulfill the promises of the past and, at the same time, to define the possibility of the future." To the young, "the old vision is dead or dying. It may inspire bitterness and outrage when it is not achieved, but it no longer animates or guides. In place of it, students (and many who are not students) are searching for a new vision, a new set of values, a new set of targets appropriate to the post-industrial era—a myth, an ideology or a set of goals that will concern itself with the quality of life and answer the question, 'Beyond freedom and affluence, what?'"

I think Keniston's analysis is not only provocative but useful as a framework within which state college faculty might speculate over the future direction of the instructional program. For instance, if Keniston is correct about the new era, with its shift away from traditional middle-class values and goals, then the state colleges, which have epitomized middle-class America, must change or find themselves increasingly irrelevant. As producers of almost half of the nation's schoolteachers, state colleges must keep abreast of changing conditions in society if, indeed, our schools are to be relevant—and we know that student unrest is now in schools as well as colleges. In short, considerable thought should be given to the implications of postindustrial society for the direction of college programs. If we are at a major turning point in our history, colleges should take the lead in helping young people define the values that will give shape and form to society. The vast quantitative expansion of our colleges has blinded us to the desperate need for qualitative improvement. At the very least we must realize what is happening. I personally believe that once the war and other immediate issues are resolved, the next campus crunch will be over the curriculum. The thrust of the future is curriculum reform. Students recently led the way to dramatic changes at conservative Brown University.

Like many students, I am long on talk and short on program. But some implications for college programs seem fairly clear. Education of the "whole man" will become more than a cliché on the front page of the catalog. There will be as much concern for the development of a student's moral, aesthetic, and creative qualities as for his rational skills—a new romanticism. His emotions and personality become important. In the jargon phrase, affective learning enters the curriculum alongside cognitive learning. *Humanistic education* is another term that is used. As part of this process, students will have a greater role in influencing the curriculum. Learning will be an active rather than a passive process and will be much more problem-oriented, hence interdisciplinary, than ever before. Independent study, group projects, off-campus activities—these will be part of an effort to involve the student more directly in what is often called *experiential education.* The general education program will hit directly at student concerns. Philosophy and religion will center on ethical and theological questions; sociology and anthropology will increasingly be crucial in helping students come to grips with fast-changing, urbanized society; the arts, from painting to film, will reflect the new aesthetic and creative interests of postindustrial America; and so the list goes. Psychology will promote personality development and open up direct personal relationships through encounter groups, sensitivity training, and other activities designed to rid individuals of inhibitions that block the way to a full and self-renewing life. There is just no doubt that this kind of nonrational involvement with other human beings is one of the paramount interests of the current student generation; it is an antidote to the alienation that seems so prevalent as the tempo of life continues to speed up. This emphasis upon quality of life will lead inevitably to interdisciplinary programs in environmental science and human ecology. (Western Washington State College is planning a second cluster college with this theme.)

Suffused throughout the curriculum will be an emphasis on problem solving, the cultivation of the ability to tackle problems not seen before—a necessity given the complexity of society and the rapid obsolescence of old knowledge as new knowledge accumulates. What is really needed is the modern equivalent of what the study of Latin and plane geometry was once supposed to have done, namely, to provide generalizable problem-solving skills applicable to whatever problems come along. I naïvely raise the question whether this is not a field worth considerably more attention than it has received, whether direct instruction in problem solving might not be feasible in addition to a problem-oriented approach within the traditional disciplines.

International education will be a concern, as indeed it is now in many state colleges. Anxious to rid themselves of provinciality, these colleges have made efforts to broaden their student body as well as their curriculum. Everywhere I went, someone was sure to mention the decreasing percentage of local students, the increase of students from other sections of the state or the country, and especially the number of foreign students. And on just about every campus there is a concern to introduce area studies as well as exchange programs that would send students abroad and bring in foreign students.

Thus far I have deliberately been talking about the impact of the new revolution in values, life style, and quality of life on curriculum planning for state colleges. But vocationalism has always been part of American education, especially in the state colleges, and it will continue to be essential. The old industrial revolution is not dead; work values and production are still necessary. A society of lotus-eaters is far from a reality at present. The goal of the state colleges must be to combine the best of vocationalism with new and imaginative programs of liberal and humane learning. Moreover, we must not forget the necessity that young people feel to complete the job of the old revolution, to see to it that all elements of our society share in the abundance made possible by the success of the industrial revolution. Nowhere is this unfinished business more evident than in the problems of our large cities. Let's take a look at the relationship of state colleges to the urban scene.

8. The Urban Crisis

People and problems are in the cities; colleges and universities are in rural areas. The founders of American colleges deliberately avoided the distractions of the city by locating their institutions where students could soak up learning in bucolic solitude. A map of the location of state colleges and regional universities would show this clearly. The standard metropolitan statistical areas include both the central cities and their surrounding suburbs. About 70 percent of our population live there, yet these areas contain only 41 percent of the institutions and 55 percent of the students (Table 23). The fact that 59 percent of the colleges and 45 percent of the students are found outside metropolitan areas reflects what has been the essentially rural orientation of American higher education.

As the socioeconomic base of the nation has shifted from the countryside to the city, so there has arisen a corresponding pressure for institutions to respond to the immense and complex needs of urban areas. The Carnegie Commission's 1968 report on federal aid *(Quality and Equality: New Levels of Federal Responsibility for Higher Education)* underlines the necessity for large sums of money to foster and strengthen existing institutional ties to the city and recommends the creation of 500 community colleges and 50 four-year colleges with a decidedly urban focus.

Clark Kerr calls for a new model to be added to our existing institutions of higher education. This new model he calls "urban-grant universities," to parallel the 69 land-grant universities which had their inception 100 years ago. The land-grant movement has been a unique feature of higher education in this country. Created basically for a rural society, these universities have made astounding contributions to American agriculture and technology and have served for years as a focal point of regional development in predominantly rural areas around the nation. They have turned their back on traditional curricula and modes of operation. In addition

TABLE 23 *Total enrollment and number of state colleges and universities by location in standard metropolitan statistical areas and by size*

1967 total enrollment	In SMSA		Not in SMSA		Total	
Less than 1,000	7,303	47%	8,233	53%	15,536	100%
Number of institutions	10	42%	14	58%	24	100%
1,000 - 5,000	127,222	32%	272,528	68%	399,750	100%
Number of institutions	44	31%	100	69%	144	100%
5,000 - 10,000	276,696	46%	326,494	54%	603,190	100%
Number of institutions	36	44%	46	56%	82	100%
Over 10,000	396,473	88%	54,122	12%	450,595	100%
Number of institutions	25	86%	4	14%	29	100%
TOTAL	807,694	55%	661,197	45%	1,468,891	100%
Number of institutions	115	41%	164	59%	279	100%

SOURCE: Compiled by Carnegie Commission on Higher Education from U.S. Office of Education data.

to performing agricultural research, these institutions, through their extension divisions, go directly to individual farmers. There has never been a question of "relevance" with regard to the programs of the land-grant colleges. *Concern, responsibility,* and *service* are words Kerr uses to describe the spirit found in these institutions. Far from the ivory tower, these places have traditionally been linked with the needs of people and of regions. The need for a parallel movement for the cities is clear.

THE RESPONSE OF AASCU INSTITUTIONS Recognizing the magnitude of the urban challenge, AASCU recently organized a task force on urban affairs. Presidents of colleges in Boston, Washington, Chicago, Buffalo, Denver, Los Angeles, Memphis, and Savannah met in the summer of 1968 to identify ways AASCU colleges could better serve the cities. One stumbling block to the coordinated development of programs has been that each institution operates with little or no information about what others are doing. As a partial remedy to this situation, *Urban Affairs Newsletter* is now being published; special projects at 90 colleges were briefly described in the first two issues.

As one would expect, inner-city teacher training receives considerable attention in a number of institutions. Special programs exist at both the undergraduate and the graduate levels. In-service education for city teachers as well as Teacher Corps and paraprofessional programs are cited. Urban studies centers are springing up, and considerable interest is shown in black studies courses and programs. Efforts to provide tutorial, enrichment, and compensatory help to elementary and secondary school youngsters are not uncommon, and recruiting programs for disadvantaged high school graduates are being developed. Some colleges provide literacy and basic education courses for adults as well as programs in health and recreation for the community. At least four colleges have recently held urban problems conferences.

A number of observations are relevant. First is the fact that many of the described programs are in colleges that are not in urban areas. Glassboro State College in New Jersey (site of President Johnson's summit meeting with Premier Kosygin) is in a decidedly rural area but offers an undergraduate program to train teachers for inner-city schools. Earlier, I mentioned Brockport, which imports children from Rochester and trains teachers for Rochester schools. In short, there is no reason why location need prohibit ties to the inner city.

A second observation is that these programs are, for the most part, special in the sense that they do not represent the main thrust of the college. One might ask whether such discrete projects represent sufficient efforts, whether substantial institutional commitment is not required if progress is to be made. There has been an accumulating educational deficit in our cities which is only now, at a time of obvious social crisis, being acknowledged. Back in 1960, Conant's *Slums and Suburbs* pointed to the "social dynamite" in the slums of the big cities. His report shocked the sensibilities of those who read it, and it received good press coverage. But little was done. The social dynamite has long since exploded. At that time big-city schools were understaffed and underfinanced; teacher training for the special problems of ghetto schools was nonexistent. The situation has deteriorated since then. One would hope, then, that these new and special programs that have been instituted at many AASCU colleges will soon become central, not peripheral adjuncts, to their programs.

A third observation is that the categories of programs and projects listed in the *Urban Affairs Newsletter* do not include all of what might be done, and probably is being done in some institutions. Readily apparent are programs to provide assistance to the public schools in the form of teacher training, educational research, curriculum development, tutoring, and enrichment programs. These activities, along with the active recruitment of disadvantaged students, could well be the thrust of the state colleges' contribution. Indeed, places like Boston State College and the District of Columbia Teachers College have for years seen their mission in this way.

But other areas for involvement exist. One is research on urban problems in health, welfare, race relations, transportation, air-water pollution, housing, municipal government, and crime. There are ample opportunities for assistance here, but faculty members traditionally find that help to local government holds neither the allure nor the financial reward that consultation and research hold at the federal level. Another important need is the vast improvement of medical care and delivery systems in our large cities. This will certainly require working out new concepts and training for doctors, nurses, and new kinds of medical personnel, along with research on medical problems and the design of new systems for delivery of health care. Still another neglected activity is training municipal employees of various kinds, including the police. A number of state colleges do train police, but much broader opportunities will have to be provided. Also important is training personnel for local industry.

Education of inner-city students, assistance to public schools, research on city problems, training of medical personnel as well as municipal employees and workers for local industries—all these are ways that institutions which properly are regional in nature could well respond to the needs of the city. No college in an urban location can be all things to all people; choices must be made. But one thing is certain: the choice *not* to be involved with the city is an untenable alternative at this juncture of our nation's history.

THE RISKS   A final observation about ties with urban problems is the fact that risk is involved with every step. Recruiting and admitting ghetto students upsets traditional "standards" and raises all sorts of questions with respect to the propriety of preferential treatment of minority students given a limited supply of places in many public institutions. As an admissions officer at Princeton University, I experienced firsthand the pressures for and against such treatment. At places like Princeton, Harvard, and Yale, at least half the freshmen applicants with SAT scores of 750 or higher (either math or verbal) are turned down to take apparently less able students but more interesting people—among them relatively large numbers of disadvantaged students, mostly black, with SAT scores well below 500. To many people this is shocking. But it is shocking only to those who equate human potential with the ability to score well on a test. Admissions officers know better, yet they are pressured to fall back on the Linus-blanket security that test scores appear to provide in order to prove to ambitious faculty that "standards" are rising. If state colleges are to enroll large numbers of inner-city youth, they must accept the fact that their admissions profiles in terms of conventional criteria will not be the same. Moreover, recruitment and admission are not sufficient; there must be carefully planned programs for inner-city students. This means commitment from the faculty, not simply pious speeches from administrators. It is clear that much of the unrest among black students stems from a lack of foresight on the part of college faculties.

The result is that, once on the campus, black students are voicing demands that challenge traditional ways of doing things — whether in admissions, curriculum, faculty hiring, or residential housing. They are no longer "grateful" for opportunities in a white man's world. There is tension at best, open conflict and violence at worst. White-taxpayer reaction, as reflected in both state and federal legislatures, is likely to cause a state college president additional sleepless nights. Any college that today seeks to expand significantly its enrollment of disadvantaged students must be ready to face tough problems. For this reason, the "readiness" program at Livingston College within Rutgers University is not to prepare students for college but to make the college ready for students.

The risk exists off the campus as well. Gone are the days when the Negro accepts what the white man says is good for him. Well-meaning, liberal white faculty members wanting to help local neighborhoods must move gingerly. There is open skepticism if not hostility among inner-city residents toward "outsiders," which includes white faculty members. "They've got nothing for us" is the feeling. Faculty members must begin by recognizing that they probably do not have ready-made solutions to city problems. These problems do not respect departmental boundaries. Interdisciplinary approaches are necessary, a fact that explains the growth of urban studies centers and other end runs around the traditional departmental structure. Research in the inner city is risky, especially for white faculty members; local neighborhoods want action, not more studies.

Colleges are facing the realities, whether on or off the campus, of confrontation politics and "nonnegotiable demands" from blacks expressing racial pride and the desire for self-determination. Trying to play safe with conventional personnel and programs infuriates the militants and, more importantly, misses the target of significant changes. Yet involvement with militant leaders, controversial issues, and unconventional programs is equally disruptive to the college, for a truly urban campus reflects all the tension and turmoil of the city itself. The point is that real involvement in the urban crisis is explosive, dangerous—and necessary. Know-how, tact, perseverance, luck, and a thick skin are required.

BLACK STUDENT DEMANDS At this point, I should note again that student unrest on state college campuses seems, by and large, to stem from black students anxious, in Keniston's terms, to complete the last stages in this country of the dispersion of power and abundance made possible by the industrial revolution. This is not SDS anarchic destruction of the "system" and should not be treated as though it were. Black student demands are usually limited in objective and related to their own particular problems and communities. For example, the Afro-American Organization at Chicago State College (23 percent of 6,000 students are black) in February, 1969, made 10 demands: black cultural center; black studies department; board of students, faculty, and community members to have full control over the cultural center; student enrollment which is representative of the racial mixture of the community; access to all college facilities for members of the community; denial of access to the college buildings to any employer who practices discrimination; college employment practices to reflect the racial mixture in the college; establishment of a student-faculty committee representative of the racial mixture in the college for hiring and firing faculty; immediate firing of racist faculty and administrators; establishment of a committee to recommend black books to the college library. The point is that whatever one's feelings about any of these demands, they and similar demands elsewhere have their roots in a genuine desire to relate the college and its program to black experience and the black community. I doubt that anyone will quarrel with this end; the quarrel has to do with the means to the end, particularly when disruption and violence are involved.

Like other institutions, state colleges are caught up in a maelstrom of conflicting forces pressing in on every side. They have done no more nor any less than other places to find answers. They are trying to make progress while maintaining order, a delicate and essential tightrope act. Student violence, whether black or white, has no place on a college campus. It must be stopped. But constructive change must take place at the same time. Treatment of the immediate symptom does not get at the cause. Ironically, the overall conservatism of the institutions and their students tends to promote change along somewhat traditional lines—adjusting admissions and curriculum but not the basic structure. One does not have to change a conservative institution very much to show progress. At a liberal university like Harvard, demands have to be far out to improve what already exists. In short, student protestors have to escalate their activities relative to the liberality of the institution if they are to show results.

The fuse to the dynamite, so far as black students in state colleges are concerned, is probably changes in admissions policy. At many of the urban colleges, students are considerably older (mid-twenties), hold jobs and middle-class work values, and are too busy for politicking. This is especially true of the evening-session students. However, as the colleges enroll larger numbers of full-time younger blacks and hard-core ghetto youths, the peace-keeping job of the president will be even more difficult. City College of New York in the spring of 1969 illustrates the point.

But let's take a look at a few state colleges and universities located in the heart of big cities to see what kinds of relationships exist between the colleges and the cities.

FEDERAL CITY COLLEGE

Federal City College in Washington, D.C., combines both the promise and the danger of an institution that dedicates itself to problems of the city. First the promise. In June of 1968, it became the nation's sixty-ninth land-grant college. Though created through existing land-grant legislation, Federal City College has the city as its focus and in this sense would appear to meet Clark Kerr's model of an "urban-grant" university. The legislation automatically means a great deal of money for the fledgling college—$7.2 million in endowment and $200,000 a year for institutional programs, as well as over $50,000 annually for extension activities. Following the land-grant example, the college has been given its marching orders to get out into the urban community. As a new institution, it is not tied to tradition, and with the designation as a land-grant institution, Federal City College is automatically pushed into the big leagues with the other land-grant universities. All this for a place that did not enroll students prior to the fall of 1968!

It opened with 2,250 commuter students, whose average age

as freshmen was about 22. About 60 percent are day students, the balance evening students. One projection calls for nearly 100,000 students served by the college in 1975—up to 20,000 regularly enrolled students, another 30,000 students served through extension and the Urban Outreach Program, and up to 40,000 students in credit or noncredit instruction through radio and television.

The college is located directly within a black ghetto area just a short distance from the Capitol. Quite clearly, Federal City College stands as a beacon of hope for the black community. The place is organized as an open-door junior college, that is, an open-door junior college with all sorts of terminal and transfer programs at the base and with upper-division and graduate programs as well. By the fall of 1968, the programs had not been worked out in much detail—and probably will not be for some time. Each faculty member was groping his way toward effective methods of reaching his students.

There will be two major programs. The first will be in-house courses leading to degrees. The goal is to suffuse the entire curriculum with urban concerns and not just restrict such activity to a department of urban affairs. Among urban-oriented courses available to freshmen are several in the social sciences—The Individual in Urban Society, Urbanization in Traditional Societies, Roots of Urban America, Introduction to Community Development, and so on. There is a humanities course called The Revolutionary Tradition. Afro-American art history is offered. First-year courses in black studies are given in History and Society in the African World, African Civilization, Uses and Techniques of Pacification, and The Politics of Dependency. Swahili is offered.

The second kind of program activity will be the land-grant extension work with direct impact upon the community. One faculty member with whom I spoke stated clearly that he and his colleagues had no illusions about the problems that they would face. His own approach is perhaps best summed up by his remark that "rationalism has run its course." By this he implies that the whole mission and structure of education in the traditional sense is bankrupt for the cities and that a totally new view is necessary. It is not exactly clear what this new view would mean, but somehow it is what Federal City is all about—an overthrow of traditional ways of doing things.

The first overthrow of tradition came with the admissions process. The place was overwhelmed with too many applicants for available spaces. Immediately the question of admissions criteria arose. Suspicious of the adequacy of conventional school grades and test scores and faced with large numbers of applicants who had been away from school for a number of years, were married, and had families and jobs, Pres. Frank Farner and his board made the first dramatic departure from tradition: they threw the names of the applicants into a hat and admitted the first class on the basis of a lottery. The first name pulled was that of a 25-year-old Negro working as a federal mailroom supervisor. He and his classmates pay $75 tuition annually.

The prospects of the college seemed promising indeed. But now danger, tension, and turmoil have gripped the place. The complexities of the situation at San Francisco State College are not readily apparent at Federal City College. The place is new and without tradition, money is available, and the first group of faculty hired were clearly committed to serving the inner city of Washington. What has happened? Black power and racial self-determination seem to lie at the heart of the matter. Some 95 percent of the students and half the faculty are black, but 75 percent of the original faculty were white. About 80 percent held the doctorate. They were a talented group paid at ·the top of the AAUP scale. But a power struggle over black separatism developed within the faculty and among some students. The struggle now is between the moderates and the militants, both white and black, who would make the college into a strident center of black power. The black studies curriculum is a central issue largely because of its militant director. Note that this turmoil is taking place largely among the faculty rather than among the students. The militant faculty members say that the college must move in their direction or the students will rebel. The administration believes that most of the students, older than typical students elsewhere, are much more moderate and are anxious to work hard and move upward in social and economic status. A militant group does control student government but is not anxious to close the place down.

The dissension within the faculty has had a strange effect on some in the moderate faction. Having come to the institution as reformers, they find themselves suddenly considered conservatives in the midst of the battle. The story is told of one man who at his former institution fought for interdisciplinary courses; he now argues for traditional offerings in the separate academic disciplines on the grounds that traditional courses are less susceptible to distortion by black power advocates. Another man calls for strict departmentalization in order to cut down the likelihood of takeover at mass meetings of the entire faculty. As I write, it is not at all clear whether Federal City College will be taken over by the separatists as a black university for black students and black faculty only or whether the more moderate group will prevail. President Farner's resignation in the spring of 1969 is an ominous sign.

METROPOLITAN STATE COLLEGE, DENVER Metropolitan State College in Denver has been in operation since 1965, enrolls 4,600 students, and aims at 25,000 by 1979! It has charted its course and is well on its way. There is nothing compromising about the purpose of the institution: "An extroverted college—no quiet, academic backwater—no cloistered halls—no ivy-covered walls—Metro Denver is Metro State's 'ivory tower.' The city is a living laboratory—the city is where the action is—MSC's basic concept of operation means complete involvement of the college and its people with the city, its people, its problems." Stressing its multipurpose nature, the college has liberal arts programs as well as applied programs in business, health services, public service, and technology. There are both two- and four-year programs for associate and bachelor's degrees. There is heavy scheduling of part-time and nighttime programs for working students. There is even a "weekend college" program for working students. Special efforts are made to recruit disadvantaged students—brown and black—and minimal admissions requirements plus low tuition and considerable financial aid provide for relatively easy access to Metropolitan State.

The college is a major component of Denver's model city program, involving itself in some 33 different parts of that program. The expectation is that the faculty and administrators of the college will be involved extensively in efforts to solve problems of the core city. "Outreach" programs involve students as well as faculty.

About 20 percent of the students are black, Oriental, Indian, and Mexican-American. The blacks and browns have the largest enrollments. Despite the obvious urban concerns of the college, there is some restiveness among all the minority groups. The Afro-American Student Organization, while endorsing much that goes on, including tuition waivers and "ethnic studies," sees the college veering away from its charted course and toward more conventional and traditional college goals. Brown students tend to feel that the college is committed to helping them. In general, there appears to be a critical but "wait-and-see" attitude among minority students. The average undergraduate is 26 years old and is probably more concerned about his education and getting ahead than with campus politics.

CALIFORNIA STATE COLLEGE, LOS ANGELES Cal State at Los Angeles sits on a hillside overlooking a very crowded area of essentially lower-middle-class people, many of them Mexican-Americans. Watts is about 5 miles away. This location is important because of the college's new commitment, represented by a faculty resolution in 1966, to what they call an *urban focus*. Actually, Cal State was established as a college of applied arts and sciences, so that it began as a vocational, service-oriented institution serving lower-middle-class people. Apparently, this original mission never really took hold because of more general needs and the pressures to emulate the University of California. The effort now is to bring the college back to this original mission with its urban focus.

The problems of Los Angeles have surrounded the college for many years, and only now are efforts being made to meet these problems. About 12 percent of the students are Negro, 6 percent Mexican-Americans, and another 6 percent Oriental—so that a quarter of the students are from minority groups. Research and public service are involved as well with the effort to get at city problems. One of the most significant of these efforts is EPIC (Educational Participation In the Community). Funded with federal money, this program enables large numbers of students at the college to participate in various kinds of community activities, including tutoring, serving as teacher aides, teaching crafts and other skills at various community centers, advising youth clubs, and supervising recreation, as well as providing assistance in hospitals and clinics and helping social workers.

At Cal State, as elsewhere, I ran into the conflict between the academic orientation of the faculty and the newly found interest in the urban scene. The tension within the institution is between those who want to do more toward meeting the needs of the community and those who would forget the exploding big-city ghetto at their doorstep to concentrate upon their research and "higher standards."

A related danger in the eyes of some is overcommitment. One professor at Cal State expressed this as a fear that the college may be overcommitting itself as to what it will do for the community and thereby may set up expectations it will not be able to realize. Grand plans of deans, administrators, and students come to naught unless faculty members are willing to do something about them.

CLEVELAND STATE UNIVERSITY
The Ohio Board of Regents has high hopes for the urban institutions that recently have become affiliated with the state system after many years as municipal institutions — Akron, Dayton, and Cincinnati. Cleveland State University is really a brand-new institution that emerged from Fenn College and is pushing ahead to establish itself as a first-rate university facing up to responsibilities resulting from its location in downtown Cleveland. The first struggle was to transform the place from a private liberal arts college to a comprehensive university. After three years, the urban focus is about to emerge. But, as at similar institutions, progress is not easy. Only 3 percent of the 10,550 students are black, despite the fact that Cleveland is 40 percent black. Reasons for the low percentage include the recent inheritance of lily-white Fenn College, heavy black enrollment in the local community college, and high attrition in the public schools and the exodus of outstanding blacks from the city to other colleges. Cleveland State is actively trying to change through an aggressive admissions policy and by having more black faculty members and administrators. Black studies is in the hands of a faculty task force.

As for militancy, there are black demands and tension is increasing. Earlier I mentioned the real dangers of student confrontation in AASCU institutions between blacks and conservative whites. Most whites at CSU are first-generation collegians and conservatives. They are not about to rally to the cause of the blacks as do white liberal students at places like Berkeley and Harvard. A blow-up at a place like CSU could be disastrous and could involve terrible physical violence. President Harold Enarson is well aware of the dangers in the situation and sees the establishment of a first-rate black studies program as one of the important solutions to a tense campus. Enarson is convinced that the university must involve itself with the city and its problems; isolation is impossible.

He comments about the financial problem of locating a new university in the heart of the city:

The eagerness for a downtown campus is motivated not by students and parents but largely by business groups, planners, advocates of downtown renewal. The university is a prime "smokeless industry" with payrolls and promises of sugar plums. But no one wants to face up to the staggering costs of raw land, high construction costs, the pitiful public transportation, and the great difficulty in building parking facilities at prices faculty and students can afford. In short, how much weight is to be given to "educational values" (need for dorm living, social interaction, etc.) and how much to the whole range of unexplored community values? The great danger is that we shall begin with great expectations (as at CSU) and then lose our nerve as we face new and very large costs. The result could be land-locked campuses with few of the amenities and with a congestion that is hostile to learning, efficiency, and good humor.

CITY UNIVERSITY OF NEW YORK Aside from Harris Teachers College in St. Louis, the City University of New York (CUNY) is the only completely municipally governed four-year institution, or set of institutions, left in the country. The other municipal institutions have been taken over partially or entirely by the state in order to meet pressing financial needs that local taxes could not provide. As it is, 50 percent of CUNY's budget comes from Albany, and Mayor John Lindsay would like to see the state pick up an even larger share. Others argue that the state should take over the City University. A budget cut of 20 percent for 1969-70 has led to university threats that admissions would be cut back. Thousands of CUNY students marched on Albany to register their protests.

CUNY consists of 15 four- and two-year colleges, a graduate center, an affiliated medical school, and a number of special research and teaching institutions and programs. The total enrollment is over 150,000. Free tuition for full-time undergraduates has been a tradition in New York City. Another tradition has been unquestioned academic excellence, particularly in the four oldest of the senior colleges: City College, Hunter, Brooklyn, and Queens. On any measure of academic quality, these institutions rate high indeed. Salaries paid to professors are among the highest in the nation. City College stands right next to Berkeley with the distinction of being the leading source of undergraduates who go on to receive doctoral degrees.

Ironically, this very tradition of high standards of scholarship within the CUNY system lies at the heart of much of the difficulty in New York City's public schools. The program of the school system has traditionally been geared to admission to the city colleges.

Progressive education never really caught on in New York City; the rigorous standards of the colleges go right on down the grades. Much of this commitment to high academic standards is undoubtedly due to the importance that the heavy Jewish population in New York has traditionally paid to education as a means of upward mobility. The irony is found in the fact that traditional scholarship and teaching methods simply are not relevant to the new population found in the city's schools. Interestingly, it now appears that the colleges rather than the schools will be the first to break up the system in order to meet the needs of black and Puerto Rican students.

Admission to the city colleges has through the years been a cutthroat business, especially recently, when places available for qualified students have been in short supply, making the competition even tougher in terms of high school grade-point average. Horror stories abound over students denied admission with, say, school averages of 82.3 when the cutoff was 82.4. In 1962, a student sued the university and won his case in a lower court on the grounds that he had received lower grades because he had taken a tougher set of courses than had others who were admitted. The appellate court, however, reversed the decision.

If funds are available, a new citywide admissions program will now make it possible for minority youths with high school averages as low as 68 to be admitted to the senior colleges, where an average of at least 82 had been required. The university board of trustees also is taking over and operating at least five of the city high schools in order to improve the education of disadvantaged youngsters. The new admissions policy in the fall of 1969 will give the university an entering freshman class that will be roughly 26 percent Negro and Puerto Rican—the same ethnic distribution found among the city's high school graduates. The next goal is more ambitious: open enrollment at CUNY for all high school graduates.

This new move is a culmination of steps begun in 1964 with what was known as the College Discovery Program and then, in 1966, the SEEK program (Search for Education, Enlightenment, and Knowledge). College Discovery students are selected in the ninth grade and assigned to one of five high school development centers for intensive college preparatory training. The SEEK program takes high school graduates who would not normally be eligible for admission and gives them special compensatory programs at the colleges themselves. This program has had very rough going at Queens College, where black students early in 1969 forced the resignation of two successive directors and demanded student control of the program. The City University also operates what are known as urban centers, which provide flexible courses of training and study for students who may go on for higher education or directly into jobs.

When it comes to assistance to the public schools, particularly in disadvantaged areas, CUNY has several programs, especially in teacher education. In the area of research on urban problems, there is a recently formed Office of Urban Studies, which pulls together university-wide efforts in a number of special research institutes and centers. CUNY has moved strongly into the health field; its recent affiliation with Mt. Sinai School of Medicine is an example. Also, through its community colleges it is producing a wide variety of paraprofessional personnel. Interestingly, in the area of training of city employees, the university has gone so far as to establish the John Jay College of Criminal Justice, a four-year institution with 2,000 undergraduates, three-quarters of whom are New York City policemen. In addition, the university is the official training agency for the New York City department of personnel. It trains municipal employees at all grades from unskilled labor up through higher levels of management. Training programs for local industry are most evident, of course, in the community colleges. And, finally, there is a great deal of student involvement in tutoring programs and other forms of community service, as I discovered during my visit to City College in the spring of 1968.

Despite the obvious commitment to the problems of the city, there remains considerable tension within the college faculty. Former Pres. Buell Gallagher at City College cites his most significant problem as that of transforming a very traditional college into one that will really respond to community needs. As he put it, how do you make a college problem-oriented rather than discipline-oriented? This question was echoed by faculty with whom I spoke: doctoral programs versus SEEK, the discipline versus the problem-oriented urban relationship. How to maintain standards but expand programs in all directions—this is the quandary.

The City University has just recently undertaken a major step forward with full doctoral programs, and faculty and departments within and among the institutions are fighting for status as the center for these programs within their discipline for the entire CUNY system. This infighting takes time and energy from other pursuits, namely, problems of the city.

The fence along St. Nicholas Terrace remains a symbol of the problem at City College. This fence is at the edge of a rather steep hill that plunges down toward the heart of Harlem below. One has the feeling that many of the faculty want to become very actively engaged with the problems of Harlem and symbolically want to tear that fence down. Nevertheless, the architecture of the place, its fortresslike appearance, and the very existence of the fence suggest the attitude of many others at City College, who clearly are worried about preserving the institution from too many concerns with the present hurly-burly of the pressing problems on every side. The tensions exploded in the spring of 1969. Student violence temporarily closed the place down as white student backlash countered black demands. President Gallagher resigned. As I write, a highly controversial dual admission plan resulting from negotiations between the college and militant students is hotly debated by students, faculty, politicians, editorial writers, and cab drivers.

Chancellor Albert Bowker has moved CUNY along on what appear to be two somewhat contradictory fronts—vastly expanded doctoral programs and, at the same time, a new commitment toward direct relationships with the needs of the city. Peter Caws, who heads the new doctoral program in philosophy, sees no conflict in principle between "duty to truth, exemplified in academic programs leading to higher degrees, research, etc., and duty to the community; indeed the university will never serve the community as it can and should if it does not constantly pay attention to the frontiers of learning in all areas."

But he does point out that there is conflict in practice, a conflict which can be resolved intelligently only by an overview of the relevance of various programs to the university. But the nub of the problem remains the faculty and precisely how, in the age of the academic revolution, they wish to spend their time. Professor Caws concludes, "If the City University were to spread out into the city and if its faculty really *cared* about the city (not just Lincoln Center), it could transform the place in a decade." What is encouraging about the CUNY system is this potential commitment—indeed, even optimism. What is discouraging is the magnitude of the task in relation to available programs.

The same can be said about all urban institutions. There seems to be some commitment, at least at the top. But the directions in which this commitment should go are not at all clear, nor are the mechanisms for expressing it. Even in the area of teacher education, a traditional concern of state colleges, there seems to be relatively little being done to make the programs relevant to ghetto schools. Totally fresh and innovative approaches in teacher education would seem the very least that state colleges might concentrate attention upon. Research and other forms of public service may be more difficult, but teacher education is an obvious place to focus institutional attention. And this focus could well be the concern of many state colleges, not just the minority found in the urban centers.

SAN FRANCISCO STATE COLLEGE Just to show how complicated things can become, let me close this chapter with a description of what has occurred at San Francisco State College. One of the lessons to be learned from campus disturbances is that there are few common denominators; uniform responses do not fit since each situation is different. To press home how complex a situation can become, I quote from G. Jon Roush of Reed College, formerly with Carnegie Corporation of New York. He spent considerable time on the San Francisco State campus over an extended period and knows the complexities as well as any outsider can.

The recent troubles at San Francisco State, even the most violent, are symptoms of a malaise with a long history. During the last ten or fifteen years, there have been three consistent sources of tension, which finally led to the disturbances of 1967-68 and the strike of 1968-69: a student body with an unusual number of student activists, a faculty and administration which felt the College was being unfairly slighted within the California system of higher education, and various strains in relations between the College and the San Francisco community.

During the late 1950s and early '60s, San Francisco State had a reputation as an interesting, urbane school. That reputation, along with the lure of San Francisco and its "beat" mystique, attracted a stream of energetic, iconoclastic students, who supplemented the majority group of quiescent commuter students. This group of unorthodox students provided some of the first members of the civil rights movement in the South in the early '60s, and in turn they attracted an increasing number of people from the movement back to State. Already skilled at organizing, they gradually developed an impressive group of student-run programs, involving both course work in the College and community action projects. These activities were financed from student body funds and were accepted, with varying degrees of understanding and commitment, by a series of indulgent and decentralized administrations.

During that period the College itself was increasingly ambivalent about its status in the California system. On the one hand, most people felt that State was a special place, with a unique ambience and one or two departments of truly national distinction. On the other hand, faculty members were conscious of the fact their counterparts across the Bay in Berkeley were paid more for teaching fewer hours, and they felt that the California Master Plan for Higher Education froze all the state colleges into second-class status by denying them Ph.D. programs and allowing the universities more restrictive admissions policies. Although the State Board of Trustees intervened rarely in the actual operation of the College until recently, seeds for distrust of Sacramento and the State Board were sown during this period. Moreover, the ambivalence persists. Many of the student radicals are conscious of the status of the College in comparison with Berkeley and Stanford; at times they will insist that State is performing the only legitimate job of education in the Bay Area, and at other times they will justify closing the school down by insisting that the education they are receiving there is worthless anyway. I have heard variations of both of those sentiments from faculty and administrators as well. It may be that many of the College's current troubles spring from a combination of injured pride and despair. Whether that is so or not, it is true that Berkeley and Stanford have been compelling models for San Francisco State, and most teachers and administrators have derived their images of their own futures from the conventional model exemplified by the two prestigious neighbors.

The third historical constant, the growing tensions between the College and the San Francisco community, is by now a familiar story for any urban college or university. The most important fact is that from the early 1960s to 1967, the black enrollment at the College declined, both absolutely and relatively, so that by 1967 black students accounted for less than 4 percent of the total enrollment of the College. At the same time that conservative citizens of San Francisco were becoming aware of State as a hotbed of radicalism, civil rights groups were beginning to question its legitimacy as a college for all people.

When the blowup did come, then, it was not surprising. The growth of black militancy on the campus and the growing student programs led to increasing demands for time, space, and money which had to be applied against a chronically stringent budget. Finally, the College administration agreed to a Black Studies curriculum leading to a degree, one of the first in the country. Money was found to hire a director for the program but for very little else. Then a special admissions program designed to admit minority-group, "underqualified" students also floundered for lack of funds after a series of bitter disputes over control. By the fall of 1968, black students felt betrayed and were laying plans for a strike.

It was in this context that George Murray, a Black Panther leader and part-time instructor at the College, made a speech off-campus advising blacks to be ready to bring guns on campus when the strike began. When he heard of the speech, State College Chancellor Glenn Dumke, a former president of the College, urged that Murray be suspended; the Faculty Senate voted to retain Murray; Chancellor Dumke then ordered President Robert Smith to suspend Murray, and President Smith complied. The intervention of Dumke and the State College Trustees was immediately seen as a denial of the College's legitimate autonomy, and it gave an impetus to the student strike which it would probably not have had otherwise. In fact, many people believed that the strike was called as a *result* of Murray's suspension. In a series of further actions, Dumke and the Trustees, with the active support of Governor Reagan, further alienated the College. The two chief episodes were the insistence that the campus be kept open, despite President Smith's opinion that a cooling-off period was needed, and the subsequent replacement of President Smith with S. I. Hayakawa. In the matter of Hayakawa's appointment especially, the faculty felt that its own role in the appointment of presidents had been peremptorily bypassed, and it seems that even if all forms had been observed, President Hayakawa would not have commanded overwhelming respect from his colleagues. The result of all of this was to unite the College as it had not been for years, and for the first time the radical students talked of the State Administration as their chief enemy rather than the local faculty and administration.

This highly polarized situation set the stage for a faculty strike. Many faculty members felt that the institution was unequivocally under attack from the outside, and although most striking faculty supported the students' demands, yet it was clear that some faculty strikers were also acting from years of accumulated bitterness of their own. For them the Trustees' interventions, the well-publicized statements from politicians, and the appointment of President Hayakawa all amounted to the last straw. Throughout the faculty strike the issues were variable and sometimes vague, and that seems to me evidence of the unfocused nature of the faculty's discontent. The persistent theme was "campus autonomy," although definitions of that phrase varied. That is not to say that the specific issues of workload and salary upon which the San Francisco Labor Council sanctioned the strike were not themselves authentically felt grievances, but these issues had an added symbolic force for those faculty who felt repressed or manipulated by the State College system.

The crisis at San Francisco State, then, revealed but did not resolve some latent problems of governance. In general, the real structure of governance for the school remains unclear because the Trustees have been unwilling or unable to clarify the limits of their own power, and their actions have been seen as whimsical and despotic. During the strike, President Hayakawa was less effective than he might have been because he suffered from a credibility gap. Striking students and faculty explicitly referred to him as a puppet taking orders from Sacramento and did not take him seriously, but on the other hand the Trustees themselves refused to enter into negotiations at all. Indeed Governor Reagan's refusal to see the strike as a situation calling for arbitration was shared by many of his critics, who also feared the effects of adopting a labor-management arbitration model. Unfortunately, because the situation was so confused by other questions, that issue was never explored very thoroughly.

If there is any single lesson to be learned from all this, perhaps it is that an urban university today will need to be a much more flexible and sensitive instrument than it has in the past, and in the case of San Francisco State that will probably require changes in the system of governance to allow for effective feedback from students, faculty and community. At State pedagogical techniques have been developed which have considerable promise for urban higher education. They include field experience in the city, decentralized action projects with academic supervision, projects designed to use the constructive skills of experienced student activists, and a number of programs designed to improve the education of San Francisco's minorities both in the public schools and in the College itself. Some of these techniques are socially risky. Some appear riskier than they are, and vice versa. But the crucial decisions concerning the College during the past two years have been made by people who are essentially uninformed about these techniques and about the people involved and who are consequently unable to weigh either the merits or the risks accurately. Until that condition changes, morale at the College will remain low, the chance for misjudgment and missed opportunities will remain high, and the College will become either moribund or more explosive.

9. Seven Years Later — Alumni

Students become alumni, and every college likes to know what its alumni are like—their careers, values, life styles, opinions of their alma mater, as well as how much money they are likely to contribute! The National Opinion Research Center in the spring of 1968 surveyed a large sample of 1961 graduates to gather such information, with special focus on their views of higher education and particularly of their own college education. The major findings of the 275-item survey will be reported in another Carnegie Commission volume. Here, let's take a look at state college alumni from 21 colleges scattered across the country and see how they compare with alumni at large (Appendix D).

Most of us parents know these state college alumni: they are the teachers of our children in the public schools. Half the 1961 graduates with jobs are in public education. (About one-quarter of alumni in *all* higher education are teachers—an amazingly high figure itself.) The sex balance is changing in state colleges now; but in 1961, consistent with feminine traditions in teacher education, a majority of the graduates were women. Most of the graduates had attended public schools themselves, and a surprisingly large number had been to community colleges.

Their occupational values, as well as training, relate to careers in education. They want to be helpful to others, and a majority want a stable and secure future. A smaller percentage of state college alumni than all alumni indicate a desire to make a lot of money. Indeed, they do not make as much money: 18 percent make over $11,000, in comparison with 29 percent of all alumni. This gap is closed if family income is used, i.e., the figures become 57 percent and 61 percent with incomes over $11,000. This is probably due to the addition of a spouse's income to the teacher's salary.

A slightly higher percentage of state college alumni than alumni in general are married. There are very few Jews among the state college graduates, and the percentage of Catholics is likewise lower than among all alumni. Protestants, especially Methodists and Baptists, are strongly represented, and there is a large group that shows no religious affiliation.

When it comes to cultural activities, state college alumni are no more active than alumni generally, in fact a bit less so. Two-fifths read nonfiction, but less than one-quarter read "serious fiction"; not many more listen to classical or serious music. Fewer than 12 percent read poetry or go to concerts, plays, or museums. These figures are, to say the least, disconcerting when one thinks of the kind of teacher he would like for his children.

Responses to questions about political and social attitudes are especially revealing. These responses clearly indicate the conservatism of state college alumni when compared with alumni in general. These are the "forgotten Americans" President Nixon referred to. A majority of the state college graduates classify themselves "conservative," whether Republican, Democrat, or Independent. They consistently give a more conservative response than alumni generally to questions about student protesting, Negro rioting, and the like. For example, 51 percent of all alumni but only 40 percent of state college alumni say that the protests of college students are a healthy sign for America. Thirty-five percent of all alumni agree that white racism is the main cause of Negro rioting; the figure is 28 percent for state college graduates, who are also somewhat less likely to agree that the federal government should make special efforts to see that members of minority groups receive a college education.

Almost 4 percent of state college alumni have experimented with drugs, but less than 1 percent would approve if their children did the same. A smaller percentage of state college graduates than alumni generally participated in either antiwar or civil rights protests, and a similarly smaller percentage would approve of their children becoming involved. In view of this fact, it is especially interesting that only 3 percent of state college alumni and 5 percent of all alumni think that today's college students are more moral than the college students seven years ago. Indeed, 10 percent of all alumni think that students are less moral than before. (Father Andrew Greeley, Catholic sociologist, says that students now in college are *too* moral for the systems available for them. A student today is likely to say that war and social injustice are more obscene and immoral than premarital sex. After just seven years, there is an obvious generation gap in the definition of morality!)

A majority of state college alumni see general education as a central purpose of college, but there is a much heavier emphasis on career training than one finds among all alumni. The state college alumni also feel that their own college faculty and administrators placed career training high on the list of institutional goals.

The alumni were asked about other goals of their own colleges and how important they seemed to the faculty and administration. Was it important, for instance, to produce a well-rounded student whose physical, social, moral, aesthetic, and intellectual potentialities have been cultivated? Half of all alumni said this was very important at their college; only 37 percent of state college alumni responded affirmatively. State college graduates consistently rated such traditional goals at their colleges as less important than did alumni generally. This list went all the way from character development to training students in the methodology of scholarship.

Alumni generally do not put their colleges in too favorable a light, but state college alumni in particular seem unimpressed by their undergraduate experience. They were just not affected as greatly by their colleges in matters like decision making, formulating values and goals, expanding tolerance for people, and so on. The alumni were asked to evaluate the caliber of classroom teaching, curriculum and course offerings, faculty, housing, caliber of the students, knowledge and professional standing of the faculty, personal contacts with the faculty. On *all* counts, state college graduates gave fewer grades of excellent than did alumni in general. Whereas 21 percent of all alumni thought the caliber of their fellow students was excellent, only 6 percent of state college alumni said so; the figures were similar with regard to the quality of the faculty.

While state college alumni wished they had more humanities courses in college, a higher percentage desired more education courses than work in the social, physical, or biological sciences. A majority wished they had studied more in college, and only one-quarter of the alumni, fewer than alumni in general, wished they had dated more.

Sixty-two percent of all alumni did *not* contribute money to their college the year before; this figure was 83 percent for the state college alumni. Indeed, fewer than a third of state college alumni belong to an alumni association. Almost a third of the alumni have never tried to interest a student in their own college.

This brings up the question of college for their own children. Almost all alumni, regardless of their own institution, want their children to go to college—and *not* to large campuses. Over two-thirds of all alumni want their children to go to colleges with enrollments under 5,000. At this point one cannot help thinking of the projected *average* enrollment of 10,000 for AASCU colleges within a decade. High academic standing and training for graduate school far exceed low costs as important factors in the choice of colleges for alumni offspring. But how important is it to the alumnus for his son or daughter to attend *his* college? Among all alumni, 18 percent say that this is important; only 12 percent of state college alumni say that it is important to them to continue the family tradition.

This implies that state college alumni do not have the same degree of loyalty to their alma mater as other graduates. This is apparently the case. Only 27 percent of all alumni consider themselves "strongly attached" to their colleges; this figure drops to 16 percent of state college alumni.

This is not a happy point at which to close this discussion of state college graduates. But what I have described may be history. State colleges are changing so rapidly in their objectives, their faculty, students, and programs that this same survey taken seven years from now may well produce very different results. At every campus I visited, there were teachers, administrators, and students anxious to build a college that has impact, that makes a difference in the lives of students. My fear is that the changes taking place may not lead to this result. They may simply ensure that the state college alumni in the next survey react no differently from alumni elsewhere—not an exciting prospect since few colleges today seem capable of much impact on the lives and values of their students. But this brings me to the "radical recommendation" of the last chapter.

10. A Radical Recommendation

The image used throughout this story of state colleges and regional universities is that of a spectrum along which these institutions are moving at various rates from single-purpose, teacher training colleges to multipurpose universities. Tremendous enrollment growth is an impetus to movement along this spectrum, and so is the pot of gold which is seen at the end of the rainbow. This pot of gold is the status, the prestige, the recognition that comes to a Harvard or a Berkeley, or at least to a University of Michigan or any one of a number of major state universities. I submit that the greatest single problem facing the AASCU membership is this question of model, of institutional purpose. The problem is reflected by the statement, "Someday we'll play in the Rose Bowl."

THE QUESTION OF MODEL Emulation of Harvard or Berkeley inevitably leads to certain steps. "Instant university" is created by simply changing the name from college to university, but often without changing much else. A visitor once asked A. Lawrence Lowell, then president of Harvard, what it took to make a great university; his answer: 300 years. University status implies graduate studies and research; the expansion of graduate programs leading to the doctoral degree becomes central to the interests of the faculty.

At the same time that this professionalization of scholarly activity takes place at the graduate level, the nature of undergraduate instruction changes. It may be an exaggeration to say that faculty members in major universities, with their interests in research, neglect undergraduate teaching. It surely is not an exaggeration to say that their interest in undergraduates stems primarily from their desire to recruit top students into their own academic fields. In short, undergraduate teaching becomes just as professionalized as what goes on in graduate school. It is for this reason that the

155

general education movement, with its emphasis upon interdisciplinary work as part of a liberal education, has largely disappeared. It is impossible to find sufficient numbers of top faculty willing to take time away from their narrow specialization for something which does not contribute to promotion within the department. All of what happens is part and parcel of what Christopher Jencks and David Riesman describe as the *academic revolution,* the overriding influence of the professionalized graduate school of arts and sciences in all phases of university activity.

With the rise to power of the academicians comes a meritocratic view of quality that places a premium on intellectual ability and academic accomplishment. Quality is equated with SAT scores and the percentage of graduates going on to law, medicine, and graduate schools of arts and sciences. The success of the college and its students becomes narrowly defined in these terms. This emphasis inevitably leads to a derogation of what James B. Conant refers to as a traditional American ideal, derived from our frontier heritage, namely, equality of status of all forms of honest labor. It leads specifically to second-class status for applied programs. Teacher education, business administration, nursing, and other applied fields show a loss in respectability. The institution becomes increasingly national in outlook rather than regional, as exemplified in its programs as well as in its recruitment of faculty and students. And with it all comes a loss of institutional coherence, warmth, and friendliness; the atmosphere changes from soft to hard.

Tensions emerge. There is a presidential power loss that parallels a faculty power gain. This is a sufficient problem in itself, but it is accentuated by a context in which institutional autonomy runs into systemwide state control and allocation of resources. A rat race develops in the scramble and competition for funds—whether from the state, federal government, or foundations. Costs soar as high-priced faculty are bought, as higher-cost graduate programs are mounted, and as libraries and computers dot the landscape. Finally, of course, the cozy college of 2,000 to 3,000 becomes a gigantic multiversity of 20,000 to 40,000 where, as Clark Kerr has said, the only common interest is the parking problem.

Most of the places I visited in the spring of 1968 showed evidence of some or all of these tensions and problems—not that all the institutions are well on the road to full university status, rather that in one way or another these places show signs of heading in that direction. It does seem disappointing for this very large group of diverse institutions to be emulating a relatively small group of prestige places. And the situation is ironic in a country which has always taken pride in diversity in higher education.

Moreover, very few of the 279 institutions about which I am writing will ever become first-rate research universities. They will not attract enough money, topflight research faculty, or academically oriented students. At present, there are anywhere from 20 to 50 major research universities, depending upon one's standards. Ninety percent of the Ph.D.'s who enter the academic world each year receive their degrees from 50 universities. To fight one's way into this group of institutions will be impossible for most. They are doomed to failure if they persist down the current road. And, in the process, they may bypass the issues which present a critical opportunity for greatness.

At this point most state college people are likely to say that I have incorrectly stated their goals. Indeed, they would say that theirs are multipurpose teaching institutions educating the middle-class backbone of the nation: teachers, businessmen, engineers, civil servants of all kinds, housewives, nurses, and so on. They would say that they are not in competition with the state university and are not especially interested in educating professional scholars, doctors, or lawyers. Many would say that they are regional in nature, meeting the needs of local students through programs designed to respond to local employment opportunities. Though these are the stated purposes, I think they are being subverted by the very nature of the system.

THE CULPRITS The stumbling block, the impediment that blocks the way toward implementation of the stated purposes of state colleges and regional universities is the academic revolution so often referred to. The graduate school and the Ph.D. are the culprits. A Ph.D. is a research degree and a union card that means acceptance among one's colleagues within the guild, the academic discipline. So long as the only source of respectable faculty is the leading graduate schools within major universities, state colleges will be automatically led toward these institutions as models. It is perfectly clear that research-oriented Ph.D.'s from these graduate schools will do all they can to transform their employing institutions into what they have just left as students. This is bound to occur despite the evidence that 85 percent of those with Ph.D.'s never publish anything after their dissertation. As these pressures mount, the trials and tribulations described in the past chapters come to pass. Above all, stated institutional purpose is never implemented. What is the solution?

There is certainly no easy one. One is tempted to say that the graduate schools must change, that Ph.D. training must somehow incorporate a knowledge about and a respect for undergraduate teaching. Indeed, people have said this for years. My own view is that basic change is unrealistic—despite student restiveness at major graduate centers—and may indeed be unwise. The academic revolution has brought with it much that is undesirable, but it has also made American scholarship second to none in the world. At the major universities, postdoctoral fellowships with accompanying research are as much a part of the academic scene as freshman instruction. The current cutback of federal research funds, if continued, not only will hurt the production of new knowledge but, perhaps more importantly, will stem the flow of many of our most creative minds into academic and scientific work. Our major universities are in many ways at the center of our national life, and the nation is increasingly dependent upon the work of men trained at the highest level of Ph.D. and postdoctoral programs. I suspect that in the future even fewer of the top Ph.D. recipients will spend much time with undergraduate teaching or with problems of their own institutions. This is not necessarily bad. As it is, only 48 percent of those who finish their degrees take academic appointments, even though 85 percent of those entering graduate school have in mind careers in teaching.

This problem presents real difficulties to emerging institutions which have to staff undergraduate courses for large numbers of students who are less than brilliant.

A NEW DOCTORAL DEGREE The time is now ripe for a major innovation in the preparation of college teachers. Predictions of a surfeit of Ph.D.'s in the 1970s underline the immediate importance of channeling large numbers of aspiring graduate students toward programs that are relevant to the teaching tasks of mass higher education. Research Ph.D. programs are an inappropriate and inefficient way to meet the faculty needs of the bulk of American institutions of higher education. My radical recommendation is that state colleges and regional universities take the lead in establishing a new and different doctoral degree specifically focusing on the preparation of undergraduate teachers, with special concern for lower-division teaching, whether in two- or four-year institutions. One thousand junior colleges enrolling 25 percent of all students in higher education are crying out for faculty members, persons with training beyond the straight master's degree but different from the research Ph.D. The market for such people would be enormous in liberal arts colleges as well. And, finally, in the emerging state colleges and regional universities there ought to be an almost limitless opportunity for such people, provided that the stated purposes of these institutions are meant to be implemented.

There has been rapid growth in the past decade of so-called intermediate degree or six-year programs, something more than a master's but less than a doctor's degree. A recent study shows that over 20 colleges and universities now claim to offer six-year programs for the preparation of college teachers, including a number of AASCU members such as Eastern Michigan University and Northern Illinois University. But the numbers of students enrolled are very small. The majority of intermediate degree programs in 116 institutions give education specialist degrees (Ed.S.) to public school personnel, often administrators and supervisory people. Secondary school teachers with master's degrees often take an additional year for the specialist degree and then move on to junior college teaching. In 1968, there were three national committees at work in an effort to come up with some common nomenclature and standards with regard to intermediate degree programs. Two national conferences on the subject have been held in Kansas City.

There are many problems in introducing a new degree for the preparation of college teachers. One is the matter of whose degree it is. Most of the specialist degrees have been under the thumb of departments or schools of education, and academic types have generally reacted negatively. Another problem is the name. At least 100 different doctoral degrees exist today, most of them recent additions in professional and applied fields. The Ph.D. remains, however, the universally recognized badge of distinction; and academicians take a dim view of any alternative, especially one with the title *doctor*. On the other hand, junior college people would rather have doctor built into the degree than to have it simply another brand of one- or two-year master's program. A few of the major universities have instituted the candidate's degree for those who, enrolled in Ph.D. programs, complete everything but their dissertations. There is a master of philosophy degree given at Yale.

The reaction of state college people to this degree is opposition because it smacks of second-class status, a consolation prize. Regardless of status, typical Ph.D. training, to my mind, is simply not appropriate to the task of undergraduate teaching and, in particular, to lower-division teaching in most colleges in this country.

Neither intermediate degrees nor truncated Ph.D. programs are the answer. There should be a new and different doctoral program and degree for the preparation of college teachers in the arts and sciences. I propose the title *doctor of arts,* which is the degree given graduates of a program begun recently in a limited number of fields at Carnegie-Mellon University and recently authorized at the University of Washington. Just as the Ph.D. is recognized as the appropriate research degree regardless of academic department, so I would hope that the doctor of arts (D.A.) might likewise become recognized as a teaching degree cutting across all academic departments. Combining the experience at Carnegie-Mellon University with my own prejudices, I see this development of doctor of arts programs proceeding somewhat as follows.

One of the strongest objections to an alternative to the Ph.D. is second-class status. The answer to this objection is that no institution should mount a program unless it is fully committed to it. Aside from the provision of sufficient resources, the specific test of commitment is the willingness of the institution not only to hire graduates of its own program but to promote them and give them tenure as well. And here is the real rub. No better test of institutional objectives can be found than to examine the criteria by which faculty are hired and promoted. The publish-or-perish doctrine is an oversimplification of what goes on in any institution, but there certainly are signs of it in many of the colleges I visited. Many times I heard a phrase to the effect that "I'm glad I got tenure years ago because I wouldn't get it now." Or a similar one, "With my Ed.D. I wouldn't be hired now; only Ph.D.'s are looked at."

If one test of commitment is that teachers trained under a doctor of arts program be considered desirable faculty members within the institution that trained them, there are clear implications for the location of these programs. The major public and private research universities would have difficulty meeting the test of commitment. Rule of thumb: Wherever there are Ph.D. programs in existence, alternative doctoral programs are not likely to work. For this very reason, well-developed state colleges, like some in

California, and regional universities with strong master's programs are the most promising places to mount doctor of arts programs. With traditions of concern about the preparation of schoolteachers, the strongest AASCU member institutions should take the lead in the preparation of college teachers. Again, some but not *all* institutions should move in this direction. In the same way, distinguished liberal arts colleges, many of which are looking for ways to expand into graduate work, might also take this route, either alone or perhaps through collaborative efforts.

As for the program itself, a number of points can be made. The doctor of arts degree represents a maximum of three years of solid graduate work. It is a degree awarded by the faculty of arts and sciences, not by the faculty of education. Heavy involvement by arts and science people is essential, not just for prestige but because at least 75 percent of the program is in academic areas. While there is heavy emphasis on scholarship, the thrust of work is applied scholarship, and the dissertation relates to curriculum and instruction at the college level. There is in-depth study of a discipline but also interdisciplinary and problem-centered approaches to general education for which at present it is almost impossible to find enthusiastic faculty. As at Carnegie-Mellon University, the educational component of the program, about 25 percent, might consist of a course in learning theory, methodology, cognition, dissertation seminar, and internship, whether in a two- or four-year college. Future faculty members should know something about teaching, the students they will teach, and the history and problems of higher education. A final and important point: the doctor of arts is a terminal degree; it is not a consolation prize for losers en route to the Ph.D., nor is it a beginning step for people aiming at the Ph.D.

The importance of active participation and concern of the arts and science faculty cannot be stressed enough. Planning a program requires the full-time service of at least one senior man in each department involved. For some, this program would entail a reorientation of their academic interest from research in their discipline to problems of curriculum and instruction in their discipline. Through this new degree program, the possibilities of close collaboration between the academic faculty and the education faculty are great. But, again, this is not an education degree; it is not the Ed.D., though the program may be similar to a few Ed.D. programs now in operation.

To say that the Ph.D. is a research degree and the D.A. a teaching degree is, of course, an oversimplification. Ph.D.'s obviously teach in our colleges and universities, and D.A.'s would presumably engage in research having to do with instruction and perhaps with traditional problems of their discipline. To say that the Ph.D. emphasizes research and the D.A. emphasizes teaching is more accurate, and this leads to the question of how a college might go about recruiting its faculty in view of the different emphases in the two degrees.

Paul Woodring of Western Washington State College has made a refreshingly direct and simple suggestion. It is to let prospective faculty members determine for themselves their role and the criteria by which they would be judged when it comes time for promotion and tenure. A scheme that makes considerable sense to me might work as follows: The institution would decide, department by department, the kind of balance that was considered desirable between faculty members whose primary strength was teaching and faculty members whose primary strength lay in research and writing. (Student input into these decisions might be very helpful.) There might be as many as three categories of positions: teacher, teacher-researcher, researcher. Having established the ratios it felt desirable, the college would then, in interviewing prospective faculty members, ask them to place themselves into one of these categories. If hired, a faculty member would periodically be asked to review his own status and desires. My guess would be that Ph.D.'s would choose the latter two categories for the most part, and this would mean teaching loads of less than 12 hours, with time for research and publication—and it would also mean that they would be judged on that basis. On the other hand, the doctor of arts people would probably choose the teaching category, and this would mean that they would carry a full 12-hour teaching schedule and that they would be promoted and given tenure on the basis of the quality of their teaching, however judged (not an easy task, I realize!).

POSSIBLE BENEFITS This combination of a different kind of college teacher devoted to the stated aims of undergraduate education and of a new system for hiring and promotion might be helpful in resolving many of the problems faced by state colleges. A direct focus upon undergraduate education would be ensured, even possibly replacing expensive Ph.D. programs and university status as a lure for ambitious faculty. At the same time the professionalization of the undergraduate curriculum would be less likely to occur and, who knows, the now meaningless phrase *liberal education* might become a reality.

If student activism today means anything, it means a revolt against professionalism divorced from the realities of life as students see them. At no time in our history has there been a greater need for a general education movement that has relevance for the hordes of young people pouring into our colleges. This means a combination of experiential and academic education that guides student energy toward constructive ends. Experimentation and innovation in the curriculum of the first two years of college are of absolute importance, and the emerging institutions ought to take the lead. So far they have not; they have instead patterned themselves in content and manner after the more prestigious institutions.

With a different kind of faculty interested in undergraduate education, unhampered by narrow academic traditions, these institutions could accomplish a great deal. Hours, credits, courses, requirements—these traditional appendages of college bureaucracy may be irrelevant. It is up to the emerging institution to plow new ground and not be content with the mechanisms of the past. Again, a new kind of faculty will be essential if there is to be anything like the kind of breakthrough in undergraduate education that is necessary. So long as institutional prestige is measured by the percentage of Ph.D.'s on the faculty, all hope is lost—especially for lower-division programs. The only alternative to a change in faculty is the equally radical suggestion that colleges and universities turn all lower-division teaching over to the community colleges.

At the same time that the need for better programs in general education is so very great, especially in the first two years, there is likewise a great need for applied programs serving local regions. In fact, regionalism seems to me one of the major justifications for any claim of uniqueness among state colleges. Again, with a new kind of faculty there would cease to be the denigration of the importance of applied programs. So long as discipline-oriented, colleague-oriented faculty from major university graduate schools are predominant, regionalism will get nowhere. Ph.D.'s have much more interest in the national scene, in their colleagues in other institutions, than they have in the local scene or in problems of their own institutions. Continuation of the present trend is bound to hurt the possibility of strong regional ties. I do not see much hope for a real commitment to urban problems in a traditionally trained faculty.

One of the disquieting signs of our time is an increasing alienation, lack of communication, lack of rapport among people. The impersonality of our large universities is well known. Different residential arrangements and other managerial schemes may help, but nothing could have as much impact on our college campuses as a faculty really concerned about the personal lives of students and the role of higher education in their development. And here, again, we need a different breed of faculty, a faculty who are in tune with the younger generation.

Finally, this focus upon a multipurpose teaching institution with strong lateral development in the introduction of new and different undergraduate programs in general education and applied areas is bound to ease the pressures upon harassed college presidents who must find funds to run their institutions. Expensive graduate work, high-priced faculty, vastly increased library holdings, large computer centers—all these require enormous sums of money and will be fought tooth and nail by the established state universities. They do not want duplication or competition, and neither does the state board as it wrestles with budgetary allocation.

TOWARD A UNIQUE ROLE Differentiation of function among institutions is the goal, and this will be possible only when faculty feel that they are indeed involved in a different kind of task. A Ph.D. at a state college will always compare his status with that of a colleague at the state university and will seek to do the same kind of things and want to receive the same kind of rewards. Thus many of the state college faculty in California feel boxed in as they look at their colleagues in the University of California. Many of them have exactly the same credentials; they want research money, graduate students, doctoral programs, university status. A change in this situation will require a change in goals.

This is not to say that no state college should become a university or offer traditional doctoral programs. There must be flexibility of opportunity provided for institutions which for one reason or another have good reason to change their function beyond that of a multipurpose college or, indeed, regional university. It has been a mistake, however, to make wholesale changes, to change the status of all institutions within a state at the same time. The fact is that every college and university has its own particular strengths and weaknesses, and all have their own rates of progress and growth; wholesale changes sacrifice individual strengths and development. The California state colleges differ markedly among themselves, just as the New Jersey colleges do.

With this flexibility should not be forgotten the vast opportunities for cooperation that the existence of new coordinating bodies at the state level provides. Major university centers with relationships moving outward to state colleges and community colleges as well as to private institutions can provide a new kind of vitality for higher education. Sharing of faculty, library, and computer resources, joint doctoral programs—these and other measures make considerable sense. Indeed, the horrendous cost of library and computer facilities makes cooperation an absolute necessity. State colleges cannot possibly exist as islands unto themselves; they must reach out one hand to the junior colleges and the other to the state universities. State colleges are vital links in the cooperation that spells better education and more efficient use of resources.

In so doing, they will find that they do not have to become self-contained giants with all the appurtenances of the major universities. I am appalled, not exhilarated, by the fantastic enrollment projections for AASCU members over the next decade, resulting in an average institutional enrollment of 10,000 students, or double the current average. Our reaction to enrollment pressure is to increase the size of existing colleges when we should be creating new ones, especially in and around urban centers. My observation is that the optimum size of a state college is between 5,000 and 10,000 students. Beyond that point, institutional solidarity, cohesion, and warmth are more difficult to maintain. Let's build new and exciting campuses in our cities rather than double the size of the colleges we now have.

In conclusion, these emerging institutions are full of vitality, enthusiasm, and dedication. What is needed is bold imagination and self-confidence to strike out in new and uncharted ways. Indeed, there should be much more emphasis on diversity; each college should aim at development of a uniqueness, its own personality. Too many state colleges look as though they had been made with the same cookie cutter. This is the matter of identity, of model. Enough has happened in higher education within recent years to convince even the most conservative educators that we haven't come close to finding answers to what education is all about. Now in a state of flux, developing state colleges can do one of two things: strike off in new directions or follow in the weary footsteps of those very places where many of the current problems are most evident. This choice should not be hard to make.

Commentary

Educational reformers and revolutionaries make much of the fact that what one learns or studies in college and what one does in one's occupational career bear at best only tangential relations to each other. They point out that on-the-job training would generally be preferable as preparation for the job and argue that colleges have a kind of monopoly in certifying people for work quite unrelated to what the college realistically teaches. An employer might respond that the ability to endure college is a test of character in the face of difficulties; the critics would in turn reply that this is what they supposed all along: college exists to teach docility and acquiescence. My own view is less harsh. I see the looseness of fit between colleges and careers as providing a certain freedom in both directions: careers need not be hemmed in by mandarin definitions and restraints; colleges can make use of the looseness of fit to develop new educational possibilities without seriously damaging the student constituency they possess while they go off in search of another constituency in addition. The colleges Alden Dunham has examined are not confined by that stern assignment of roles that is the fate of postsecondary nonuniversity institutions in many Continental countries.

These colleges began for the most part as teachers colleges, and though most have now become multipurpose state colleges or even universities, they may still send from half to 70 percent of their students into teaching. But this figure itself is misleading if it is not also noticed what proportion of these are going into elementary and what proportion into secondary education, for this affects the sex ratio of the college and ordinarily this also affects its status. By the time such a college recruits as many men as women and sends a third or more of its students into careers other than education, it is likely that even more dramatic changes will have occurred at the administrative and faculty levels. The president is apt to have a Ph.D. in history, as Glenn Dumke did when he became president of San Francisco State College, or to be a political scientist (like President James W. Miller of Western Michigan University), rather than having his doctorate in education. In the example of the State College at Brockport, New York, Alden Dunham lays out the anatomy of the shift toward a departmentalized faculty in the arts and sciences which has gone on dramatically just in the last several years. In some instances such a drastic change—as in the State University at Albany—has been traumatic for particular departments where men and women who have devoted their lives to preparing teachers find themselves suddenly devalued or under-employed when the mission changes. But Brockport's overall growth has been so rapid and faculty salaries so newly splendid as to assuage resentments among the holdover faculty, for innovation is always easier when it does not involve redistribution of scarce resources. While, as the realtors might say, Brockport has been tipped in the direction of the liberal arts and perhaps eventually of Ph.D. programs, it now turns out more schoolteachers than it did before, because of its absolute growth in size.

Yet in the overall plan of the State University of New York, Brockport is not a major university center, that prerogative being confined to Buffalo, Albany, Binghamton, and Stony Brook. Alden Dunham has the same impression that I do, namely, that the New York state colleges are as yet not envious of these four state universities. California stands in sharp contrast where the Master Plan of 1960 forbids even such large and distinguished state colleges as San Diego State, or San Jose State, or San Francisco State to give the doctorate or to call themselves universities—one element in the move of their faculties toward unionization and perhaps toward radicalization. But of course New York's turn may come later—the situation is partly ameliorated by the fact that except at Buffalo there is no state university in the same city as a state college, unlike the situation in California.

In New York and, in general, in the Middle Atlantic and New England states, public higher education has been a stepchild in comparison with elite private higher education; since the public institutions are such latecomers (with notable exceptions like the New York city colleges), they have been more grateful for recent advances than bitter about status disparities among themselves. However, where the state university is the leading institution, resentment can be focused against it by the less elite state colleges and regional universities who can fall back both on intrastate regionalism and an all-American Populism. East Carolina College in Greenville, North Carolina, can become a university (and even lay claim to a medical school), in part by harnessing the feeling that Chapel Hill is subversive, and is certainly not the place where "forgotten Americans" can go for their nonsnobbish down-to-earth curricula. The University of South Alabama can harness similar antagonisms vis-à-vis the University of Alabama and to a lesser degree vis-à-vis Auburn, the land-grant college. The regional universities of Texas can point to the student ferment at the law school and elsewhere at Austin, right under the legislators' noses, as a basis for increasing their own appropriations relative to that of the major university system.

This kind of battle is of course not new: Michigan State used its county agents, so to speak, as counters to Ann Arbor's lawyers and its Grosse Pointe elites. Now Michigan State itself, as Dunham points out, suffers from the forays of the regionals on the move. Indeed, this progression has some of the qualities of bureaucratic succession in a totalitarian society, as when under Stalin a group of bureaucrats would come into power by denouncing their superiors, only in turn to be sent to Siberia. It goes without saying that this analogy overdramatizes enormously the succession crises of state university systems. But it is perfectly clear that the development of the colleges Alden Dunham describes is in the direction of more upper-division and graduate students and, therefore, a proportionately larger faculty who get paid more for doing (in teaching time) somewhat less. The development, in other words, is from mass production of undergraduate degrees—or even less expensive dropouts—toward class production of upper-division academic majors, specialist undergraduate programs, and fantastically expensive graduate programs, or handicraft production.

These developments in turn depend on what seems to me the basic strategy of pyramiding in American public education, comparable to the procedure by which holding companies used to operate prior to the New Deal. This pyramiding involves formulae for faculty-student loads calculated on the basis that those who teach graduate students have a span of control of about 1 to 4, whereas those who teach freshmen have a span of control closer to 1 to 20. But in order to teach graduate students without an enormous endowment or subsidy, one has to have a captive audience of undergraduates to provide teaching assistant jobs for the graduate students, or at least for a large number of them. That is why the effort toward which some of these institutions are pointing, of reducing to the vanishing point their freshman and sophomore years, seems doomed to failure, even though a few experiments along this line may perhaps succeed. Correspondingly, few, if any, of these upwardly mobile institutions have reached the point of that devotion to undergraduate teaching that one can find in a few of the most eminent universities, such as Princeton or California Institute of Technology, where some of the cosmopolitan, research-minded faculty are willing to offer freshman seminars and other work for as yet unspecialized undergraduates, so that it is sometimes the graduate students who feel neglected.[1]

Seen as colleges in transition, the institutions Alden Dunham describes are then, in many cases, seeking a new, more prestigeful academic mission without being either able or willing to surrender preexisting missions. The fight goes on as to the appropriate missions, not only among the different segments of the state system (should Brockport get a law school although the State University of Buffalo has one?) and between the more research-minded and recent and the more service-minded and usually older faculty within an institution, but also within faculty members themselves, reflecting the ambivalence as to goals characteristic of the strains and pulls within the academic professions.[2] Contrary to widely prev-

---

[1] It is often said in these institutions that the undergraduates are more fun to teach. One now-retired Harvard don who shared this preference used to declare that he might discover among his undergraduates a new John F. Kennedy or a Robert Oppenheimer. Virtually no state colleges and universities have the power to restrict enrollment at the undergraduate level that a private institution has, which can offer its faculty a hand-picked student generation from which the academically untalented and increasingly the extravagantly "collegiate" students have been eliminated. Some of the major state and land-grant universities have sought to do the next best thing and to group their bright students, of whom they have a large number, in honors colleges or programs, making them available in this way to each other and to selected faculty; Michigan State University, for example, has made a nationwide effort to recruit National Merit scholars or finalists and to provide such options for them.

[2] For a survey report on the goals of academicians, see Edward Gross and Paul V. Grembsch, *University Goals and Academic Power,* American Council on Education, Washington, 1968; see also forthcoming work by Talcott Parsons and Gerald Platt concerning the balance of faculty members' desires between teaching, research, and administration; and Joseph Gusfield, David Riesman, and Zelda Gamson, *Faculty Cultures and Popular Education,* Doubleday, New York, 1970, chap. 13.

alent stereotypes, most professors would not choose posts where they did *only* research; they want some teaching, and the ambivalence concerns the sort of students whom they are willing or eager to teach. For example, some of the same California state college faculty members who are bitter that they cannot themselves train doctoral students—for do they not hold doctorates themselves from leading institutions?—are among the most insistent about the responsibility of the state colleges to recruit larger numbers of black, Mexican-American, and other usually less adept students: they want some of the mission of the university as well as some of the mission of the community colleges. It is true that they might not want much of the latter mission very long, at least for themselves, for it may look more romantic and idealistic from afar than close at hand. And it may also be true that some of them unconsciously chose the state college as a place to settle down rather than the university because they did not want to be faced with the competitive pressures, and perhaps with the intradepartmental rivalries, they found in their own graduate work at Berkeley or Columbia.[3]

What I am saying here is that the competing political and cultural pressures in America between elitism and Populism, selectivity and the open door, give many academicians ambivalent feelings about the maintenance of standards. "Standards" implies exclusion and hence cultural hegemony. Social-class and even revolutionary antagonisms in such countries as Japan and France have not deprived the national high culture of its hegemony: resistance

[3] The California state colleges have the additional mixed blessing in many but not all instances of being in one of America's prime vacation lands; some of their resentful faculty, as their critics have noted, prefer the Bay Area or San Diego to the lower salaries and hotter summers of the University of Kansas (an academically distinguished university) or the cold winters of topflight Minnesota. They want the institution that suits them scenically, and that is in a place where they wish to bring up their children, to adapt itself to their academic values, whatever the framers of the Master Plan may have thought about it in 1960.

Furthermore, there is probably a subtle difference as to what is considered a publication in one of the country's major universities, a member of the elite Association of American Universities, and a publication-minded member of the Association of State Colleges and Universities. In some of the latter, a nonoriginal text, an article or book review in the local paper, an address at an annual meeting, may count as a publication. At the lower levels of academic excellence, quantity has not yet changed into quality. That such change does occur at the higher levels seems established by studies of Stephen and Jonathan Cole at Columbia concerning the difference between those who publish often and those who publish fewer things that count for more in terms of influence. The low-quality high producers don't get too far in the better departments.

is apt to take the form of a rather abstract class rancor, and in addition, it is not bound up with the antagonism of young men to being taught by school marms, of blacks to being taught by whites, or of "forgotten Americans" to being taught by Eastern-style snobs. The gatekeeper strategies in "open-door" admissions policies often go on outside the full awareness of individual faculty members. Indeed, within their own classes, including small seminars, many faculty members do not see the actual students in front of them but rather that visible front organization that presents itself as "the students" who, I would surmise, are ordinarily somewhat above average in energy and aptitude. One might even contend that a certain amount of poor communication and distorted feedback may be necessary if faculty are to maintain their morale in the face of an ennervating environment of mediocrity.

Nevertheless, although faculty members may allow themselves a somewhat limited sense of the students in their classes, they are often inclined to deprecate the impact of their colleges on the undergraduates whom they see as coming for a job and a good time, finding both, and emerging relatively unaffected.[4] I have always been skeptical of the view that college has a minimal impact on students' values in the light of the massive public opinion data that show that education is the greatest single dividing line for cultural and political attitudes. The growth of tolerance and the decline of ethnocentrism among college students may not reflect their courses so much as it does their widening orbits of permitted associates—but this very widening is legitimated and supported by the faculty's values.[5]

Alden Dunham is aware (see Chapter 7) of the changes in student temper, and he sees the colleges as losing touch both with

---

[4] In their typology of students, Burton Clark and Martin Trow distinguish between the vocationally oriented students and the collegiate ones; with rising affluence, these two cadres tend more and more to overlap, so that students coming to college to become schoolteachers or accountants are tending to shed the lower-middle-class inhibitions as they move into that postindustrial world described in Alden Dunham's quotations from Kenneth Keniston's work. As the latter suggests, the eager striver who rejects the frivolities of college is sometimes to be found among black undergraduates—for example, one can see them at Federal City College in Washington, D.C., although in most of the established Negro colleges, the collegiate and the vocational overlap as they do elsewhere.

[5] For a discerning discussion and summary of research on this controversial issue, see Kenneth A. Feldman and Theodore M. Newcomb, *The Impact of College on Students,* Jossey-Bass Publishers, San Francisco, 1969.

their older constituencies, who are concerned that there be enough elementary school teachers or teachers of handicapped children, and with the newer, more hedonistic student generation which demands relevance, participation, and affective learning. He has compassion for the former, that is, the older constituencies; but his own real sympathies seem to lie with the latter, with the fore-runners who express the presently widespread student attitudes. He would like to see the colleges respond to the emotional pre-occupations among their students, which I would grant are gener-ally more humane than the older frivolous (and at times brutal) collegiate styles of relation which can still be found among men and women and among same-sex groups on the campus. Even so, I hesitate to get the colleges more involved than they already are be-coming in these subtle emotional areas, especially since it seems to me that the students are not generally underprivileged in the atten-tion bestowed upon interpersonal relations, whatever may be miss-ing in the quality and intensity of those relations. The students do want sensitivity training; T-groups, Esalen-type seminars, Bethel-type interpersonal laboratories are common on both coasts, though unevenly available in the Midwest and South. Sensitivity training may come as a liberation to the inhibited lower middle class, but because of the heterogeneity of the state colleges, I can imagine that it is often conducted in such a way as to manipulate the inhibited for the benefit of the sophisticated, the intrusive, and the sadistic. Of course, this need not happen; but it is no tool to be blithe or cas-ual about. Faculty can harm students in a class on calculus or seventeenth-century British history or in any other field; but on the whole, the young are better defended from adults than from each other; and there may be slightly less risk in the effort to trans-mit skills and competences and heritages than, for example, in an effort to persuade the vulnerable that their shyness is a hangup. My real concern is that the students in state colleges, and indeed in many elite universities, may not be stretched to the limit of their powers in any respect at any time. This may especially be so for the able, who have learned early how to get by on little work. (I would like to see much more intensive work in the arts, and here agree entirely with Alden Dunham.)

During a brief, intense, and stimulating visit to San Diego State College last May, I found that many students took the positions Al-den Dunham describes, saying that they should not attend college simply for credentials, should have pass-fail so that they did not work for grades, and should have student-directed or -initiated courses in sensitivity training and other affective areas. I said I would respect such demands if the students were willing to immerse themselves in a foreign language and culture (as in some types of Peace Corps training) or if they were prepared to study at the pace at which, let us say, Reed College students studied, if only for a spell. They thought my view elitist and rejected the idea that there might be differences in the educational reforms needed at Reed College and San Diego State.[6]

What I do fear is that reforms spread rapidly from one place to another without regard to the distinctions of locale that Alden Dunham has mapped. Thus urban studies programs are spreading. I often marvel at the puffery that goes into what colleges say about what they do in this and other fields. Alden Dunham's behavioral measure of playing tennis with the best local player at state college needs to be applied to these novel programs also to see to what extent they live up to their blurbs. I believe it is extremely difficult to create even a single good interdisciplinary course and that its half-life is likely to be short. A whole new program—that would be magic.

Such misgivings take us back to the theme at the outset of this Commentary concerning the loose articulation between the work people do in later life and what they learn in college. Alden Dunham speaks about learning the techniques of problem solving, and it may be that there are techniques which are applicable across a range of problems and that can be learned: a systems approach. But before we abandon even our creaky curricula, I would want to be surer than I am as to how such an approach would assist the heterogeneous populations of these very divergent institutions. I do not see history as being taught this way, nor the arts. I see the faculty as riding one set of merry-go-rounds and the students another set; my hope is that there will be some swings in which semiconnection takes place and that students will begin what Gregory Bateson calls deutero-learning, learning how to learn, which in some fields may

[6] San Diego State is a very large and complex institution as Alden Dunham makes clear, and I refer in the text to only one aspect of my discussions there. I met a number of graduate students in various master's programs who seemed to me exceptionally qualified and who were benefiting from the fact that they had an excellent faculty to turn to who had no Ph.D. candidates to put the master's candidates in the shadow. The undergraduates I met were also extremely various.

be termed problem solving. The difference of degree between Alden Dunham and me reflects a difference as to the kinds of impact that criticism will have on the more defensive people in the state colleges: will it incite or inspire them to create the dramatically new curricula that Alden Dunham envisages, or will it make them even more defensive about their relatively low status vis-à-vis the academic elite? I fear that much criticism by highbrows of the public schools has the latter effect, and hence may be self-defeating. At the levels about which Alden Dunham is writing, I am less sure of this. But I always want to be sure about what will take the place of out-of-date curricula and of the relatively untransformable people now teaching them when the effort is made to install new ones. This is why the indiscriminate attacks on admittedly feeble and indefensible academic practices trouble me. Criticism by radicals of powerful institutions need not propose alternatives; criticism of weak and spongy institutions is something else.

To be sure, Alden Dunham on the road was constantly meeting faculty as well as student journalists and other leaders who complained about the lack of radicals and bemoaned the apathy of the great majority of students in the state colleges. My own view, as already implied, is pluralistic: I would like to see students with some intense preoccupation about a great variety of curricular and extracurricular interests; but I question the moral chauvinism that assumes that people who do not share one's own crusades are therefore somehow ethically and psychologically inferior.[7] This attitude is akin to the one which Alden Dunham criticizes throughout this volume, namely, that there is only one monolithic model of academic success based on those leading universities which emphasize research and graduate training. He notices that programs at Western Michigan University geared to the state's industries can have quality and distinction, even though they do not award the Ph. D., and he singles out Weber State College in Ogden, Utah, because of a teacher training program that is innovative. He discusses the merits of the doctor of arts degree which would focus on ability as a teacher-scholar. What he is saying over and over is that we have enormous apparent diversity in American higher education, but little genuine pluralism of esteem.

Among graduate students, especially in the humanities and the

---

[7] Concerning the "anti-apathy crusade" see my comments in *Faces in the Crowd* Yale University Press (paperback edition), New Haven, 1965, pp. 37 - 38.

social sciences, and precisely at the elite universities, there is spreading a revulsion against research—often against research as such, all of which appears to be geared to careerism, to the war machine, or simply to preparing young people to enter the labor force in an industrious and willing fashion. However, I doubt whether the colleges of the forgotten Americans will greatly profit from a new cadre of teaching-oriented candidates. For one thing, affectively oriented teaching, unsublimated by scholarship and research, runs the risk, at least for its more talented devotees, that if they do not win student disciples and closeness, they have nothing else to turn to, to justify their lives. For another, the "ordinary" state colleges will lose out to the glamorous ones like San Francisco State, Old Westbury, or (de facto black) Federal City College.

This intensified concern of elite students and some faculty for undergraduate teaching coincides with the conclusion of Governor Ronald Reagan and other Conservative or Right-wing politicians that if faculty would only get out of their consulting and their trivial or pretentious research and back into the classroom, the turbulent students would become quiet again. In several states, bills have been introduced into the legislature to require state college and university employees to teach a certain minimum number of hours, such as 12—an ironic commentary on the efforts to reduce hours in the California State Colleges to the 6 or less of the State University system.

Correspondingly, it seems quite possible that what will suffer in the coming years, both from the Left inside and the Right outside the universities, are those more esoteric functions which cannot defend themselves in the Populist forum and which depend on patronage and protection and privilege if they are to flourish.[8] Those colleges are best protected in the immediate years ahead which have moved relatively least from a base in teacher education and other applied fields. Schoolteachers (unlike some eminent professors) are individually weak, but they have collective strength in the statehouses of the country, where they can lobby for the budgets of their training institutions and protect these by requiring certification before anybody can be licensed to teach in the public schools. (Some otherwise comparable professions, such as engineering, lack the power to enforce certification on employers, thus attenuating the tie between formal schooling and employabil-

[8] See Martin Trow, "Urban Problems and University Problems," paper delivered at All-University of California Conference, Riverside, March, 1969.

ity.) To be sure, in competition with the junior colleges, which Christopher Jencks and I in *The Academic Revolution* termed safe colleges, the four-year colleges and universities described in this volume are more exposed to student pressure and community backlash. [9]

In what has been said, I have made clear that the current hostility against the more advanced and esoteric functions of the great universities gains its momentum from the Left as well as from the Right and from traditional American philistinism. From all sides the notion has spread that the function of professors is to serve the society directly and immediately: by teaching the young, by responding to them as whole persons, and by responding to society's problems as whole problems rather than as refracted by the academic disciplines. Quite apart from the question as to whether either people or problems are always best served directly, without the intervention of protections and paradigms that may advance as well as delay results, it is important to recognize without cynicism the fact that all occupations and professions must serve the people in them as well as the clients of those people. Inevitably, there will be some strain and tension here, and the wants of a profession can become a baroque edifice over the orginal needs that gave rise to the calling in the first place. I like to think of the great state universities as the cathedrals of an apparently secular age; and if the cathedrals are often uncomfortable, even for their inhabitants, life would be poorer for all but the very poor without them—and even the very poor would not be better off (save as a momentary sop to their resentment) if they were razed.

David Riesman

---

[9] In specific locales, of course, there are exceptions either way here. Fresno State College is "safer" than Merritt College, a de facto black college in Oakland, California, or San Mateo College, another two-year college with some black students in the Bay Area. Cortland State College, which is in the same league but not as far along as Brockport, in upstate New York, is probably "safer" than some of the new community colleges in the New York metropolitan area; even commuter junior colleges can become explosive with the proper mixtures of ethnicity and race.

Appendix A: AASCU Membership List

Alabama

Alabama College
Montevallo, Alabama 35115

Alabama State University
Montgomery, Alabama 36101

Florence State University
Florence, Alabama 35630

Livingston State University
Livingston, Alabama 25470

Troy State University
Troy, Alabama 36081

University of South Alabama
Mobile, Alabama 36608

Arizona

Northern Arizona University
Flagstaff, Arizona 86001

Arkansas

Arkansas A & M College
College Heights, Arkansas 71633

Arkansas Polytechnic College
Russellville, Arkansas 72801

Arkansas State University
State University, Arkansas 72467

Henderson State College
Arkadelphia, Arkansas 71923

Southern State College
Magnolia, Arkansas 71753

State College of Arkansas
Conway, Arkansas 72032

California

California State College
at Bakersfield
Bakersfield, California 93304

California State College
at Dominguez Hills
Gardena, California 90247

California State College
at Fullerton
Fullerton, California 92631

California State College
at Hayward
Hayward, California 94542

California State College
at Long Beach
Long Beach, California 90804

California State College
at Los Angeles
Los Angeles, California 90032

California State College
at San Bernardino
San Bernardino, California 92407

California State Polytechnic College
Pomona, California 91766

California State Polytechnic College
San Luis Obispo, California 93401

Chico State College
Chico, California 95927

Fresno State College
Fresno, California 93726

Humboldt State College
Arcata, California 95521

Sacramento State College
Sacramento, California 95819

San Diego State College
San Diego, California 92115

San Fernando Valley State College
Northridge, California 91324

San Jose State College
San Jose, California 95114

Sonoma State College
Rohnert Park, California 94928

Stanislaus State College
Turlock, California 95380

Colorado
Adams State College
Alamosa, Colorado 81101

Colorado State College
Greeley, Colorado 80631

Metropolitan State College
Denver, Colorado 80204

Southern Colorado State College
Pueblo, Colorado 81005

Western State College of Colorado
Gunnison, Colorado 81230

Connecticut
Central Connecticut State College
New Britain, Connecticut 06050

Eastern Connecticut State College
Willimantic, Connecticut 06226

Southern Connecticut State College
New Haven, Connecticut 06515

Western Connecticut State College
Danbury, Connecticut 06814

District of Columbia
District of Columbia Teachers College
Washington, D.C. 20001

Federal City College
Washington, D.C. 20001

Florida
Florida A & M University
Tallahassee, Florida 32307

Florida Atlantic University
Boca Raton, Florida 33432

Florida Technological University
Orlando, Florida 32801

University of West Florida
Pensacola, Florida 32504

Georgia
Albany State College
Albany, Georgia 31705

Armstrong State College
Savannah, Georgia 31402

Augusta College
Augusta, Georgia 30904

Columbus College
Columbus, Georgia 31907

Georgia College at Milledgeville
Milledgeville, Georgia 31061

Georgia Southern College
Statesboro, Georgia 30459

Savannah State College
Savannah, Georgia 31404

Valdosta State College
Valdosta, Georgia 30601

Guam
University of Guam
Agana, Guam 96910

Idaho
Boise State College
Boise, Idaho 83707

Idaho State University
Pocatello, Idaho 83201

Illinois
Chicago State College
Chicago, Illinois 60621

Eastern Illinois University
Charleston, Illinois 61920

Illinois State University
Normal, Illinois 61761

Northeastern Illinois State College
Chicago, Illinois 60625

Northern Illinois University
DeKalb, Illinois 60115

Western Illinois University
Macomb, Illinois 61455

Indiana
Ball State University
Muncie, Indiana 47306

Indiana State University
Terre Haute, Indiana 47809

Iowa
University of Northern Iowa
Cedar Falls, Iowa 50613

Kansas
Fort Hays Kansas State College
Hays, Kansas 67601

Kansas State College of Pittsburg
Pittsburg, Kansas 66762

Kansas State Teachers College
Emporia, Kansas 66801

Wichita State University
Wichita, Kansas 67208

Kentucky
Eastern Kentucky University
Richmond, Kentucky 40476

Morehead State University
Morehead, Kentucky 40351

Murray State University
Murray, Kentucky 42072

Western Kentucky University
Bowling Green, Kentucky 42102

Louisiana
Francis T. Nicholls State College
Thibodeaus, Louisiana 70301

Grambling College
Grambling, Louisiana 71245

Louisiana Polytechnic Institute
Ruston, Louisiana 71271

McNeese State College
Lake Charles, Louisiana 70602

Northeast Louisiana State College
Monroe, Louisiana 71201

Northwestern State College
Natchitoches, Louisiana 71457

Southeastern Louisiana College
Hammond, Louisiana 70402

Maine
Arroostook State College
Presque Isle, Maine 04769

Farmington State College
Farmington, Maine 04938

Fort Kent State College
Fort Kent, Maine 04743

Gorham State College
Gorham, Maine 04038

Maine Maritime Academy
Castine, Maine 04421

Washington State College
Machias, Maine 04654

Maryland
Bowie State College
Bowie, Maryland 20715

Coppin State College
Baltimore, Maryland 21216

Frostburg State College
Frostburg, Maryland 21533

Morgan State College
Baltimore, Maryland 21212

St. Mary's College of Maryland
St. Mary's City, Maryland 20686

Salisbury State College
Salisbury, Maryland 21801

Towson State College
Baltimore, Maryland 21204

Massachusetts
Boston State College
Boston, Massachusetts 02115

Bridgewater State College
Bridgewater, Massachusetts 02324

Fitchburg State College
Fitchburg, Massachusetts 01420

Framingham State College
Framingham, Massachusetts 01701

Lowell State College
Lowell, Massachusetts 01854

Massachusetts College of Art
Boston, Massachusetts 02215

Massachusetts Maritime Academy
Buzzards Bay, Massachusetts 02532

North Adams State College
North Adams, Massachusetts 01247

Salem State College
Salem, Massachusetts 01970

Westfield State College
Westfield, Massachusetts 01085

Worcester State College
Worcester, Massachusetts 01602

Michigan
Central Michigan University
Mt. Pleasant, Michigan 48858

Eastern Michigan University
Ypsilanti, Michigan 48197

Ferris State College
Big Rapids, Michigan 49307

Grand Valley State College
Allendale, Michigan 49401

Lake Superior State College
Sault Ste. Marie, Michigan 49783

Northern Michigan University
Marquette, Michigan 49855

Minnesota
Bemidji State College
Bemidji, Minnesota 56601

Mankato State College
Mankato, Minnesota 56001

Moorhead State College
Moorhead, Minnesota 56560

St. Cloud State College
St. Cloud, Minnesota 56301

Southwest State College
Marshall, Minnesota 56258

Winona State College
Winona, Minnesota 55987

Mississippi
Alcorn A & M College
Lorman, Mississippi 39096

Delta State College
Cleveland, Mississippi 38732

Jackson State College
Jackson, Mississippi 39217

Mississippi State College for Women
Columbus, Mississippi 39701

Mississippi Valley State College
Itta Bena, Mississippi 38941

University of Southern Mississippi
Hattiesburg, Mississippi 39401

Missouri
Central Missouri State College
Warrensburg, Missouri 64093

Harris Teachers College
St. Louis, Missouri 63103

Missouri Southern College
Joplin, Missouri 64801

Missouri Western College
St. Joseph, Missouri 64501

Northeast Missouri State College
Kirksville, Missouri 63501

Northwest Missouri State College
Maryville, Missouri 64468

Southeast Missouri State College
Cape Girardeau, Missouri 63701

Southwest Missouri State College
Springfield, Missouri 65802

Montana
Eastern Montana College
Billings, Montana 59101

Northern Montana College
Havre, Montana 59501

Western Montana College
Dillon, Montana 59725

Nebraska
Chadron State College
Chadron, Nebraska 69337

Kearney State College
Kearney, Nebraska 68847

Peru State College
Peru, Nebraska 64821

Wayne State College
Wayne, Nebraska 68787

New Hampshire
Keene State College
Keene, New Hampshire 03431

Plymouth State College
Plymouth, New Hampshire 03264

New Jersey
Glassboro State College
Glassboro, New Jersey 08028

Jersey City State College
Jersey City, New Jersey 07305

Montclair State College
Upper Montclair, New Jersey 07043

Newark State College
Union, New Jersey 07083

Paterson State College
Wayne, New Jersey 07473

Trenton State College
Trenton, New Jersey 08625

New Mexico
Eastern New Mexico University
Portales, New Mexico 88130

Western New Mexico University
Silver City, New Mexico 88061

New York
State University College
Brockport, New York 14420

State University College
Buffalo, New York 14222

State University College
Cortland, New York 13045

State University College
Fredonia, New York 14063

State University College
Geneseo, New York 14454

State University College
New Paltz, New York 12561

State University College
Old Westbury, New York 11568

State University College
Oneonta, New York 13820

State University College
Oswego, New York 13126

State University College
Plattsburgh, New York 12901

State University College
Potsdam, New York 13676

State University College
Purchase, New York 10577

State University of New York
at Albany
Albany, New York 12203

State University of New York
at Buffalo
Buffalo, New York 14214

North Carolina
Appalachian State University
Boone, North Carolina 28608

Asheville-Biltmore College
Asheville, North Carolina 28800

East Carolina University
Greenville, North Carolina 27835

Elizabeth City State College
Elizabeth City, North Carolina 27909

Fayetteville State College
Fayetteville, North Carolina 28301

North Carolina College
at Durham
Durham, North Carolina 27707

Pembroke State College
Pembroke, North Carolina 28372

Western Carolina University
Cullowhee, North Carolina 28723

Winston-Salem State College
Winston-Salem, North Carolina 27101

North Dakota
Dickinson State College
Dickinson, North Dakota 58601

Mayville State College
Mayville, North Dakota 58257

Minot State College
Minot, North Dakota 58701

University of North Dakota—
Ellendale Center
Ellendale, North Dakota 59436

Valley City State College
Valley City, North Dakota 58072

Ohio
Bowling Green State University
Bowling Green, Ohio 43402

Central State University
Wilberforce, Ohio 45384

University of Akron
Akron, Ohio 44304

Youngstown State University
Youngstown, Ohio 44503

Oklahoma
Central State College
Edmond, Oklahoma 73034

Northeastern State College
Tahlequah, Oklahoma 74464

Southeastern State College
Durant, Oklahoma 74701

Oregon
Eastern Oregon College
La Grande, Oregon 97820

Oregon Technical Institute
Klamath Falls, Oregon 97601

Southern Oregon College
Ashland, Oregon 97520

Pennsylvania
Bloomsburg State College
Bloomsburg, Pennsylvania 17815

California State College
California, Pennsylvania 15419

Cheyney State College
Cheyney, Pennsylvania 19319

Clarion State College
Clarion, Pennsylvania 16214

East Stroudsburg State College
East Stroudsburg, Pennsylvania 18301

Edinboro State College
Edinboro, Pennsylvania 16412

Indiana University of Pennsylvania
Indiana, Pennsylvania 15701

Kutztown State College
Kutztown, Pennsylvania 19530

Lock Haven State College
Lock Haven, Pennsylvania 17745

Mansfield State College
Mansfield, Pennsylvania 16933

Millersville State College
Millersville, Pennsylvania 17551

Shippensburg State College
Shippensburg, Pennsylvania 17257

Slippery Rock State College
Slippery Rock, Pennsylvania 16057

West Chester State College
West Chester, Pennsylvania 19380

Rhode Island
Rhode Island College
Providence, Rhode Island 02908

South Dakota
Black Hills State College
Spearfish, South Dakota 55783

General Beadle State College
Madison, South Dakota 57042

Northern State College
Aberdeen, South Dakota 57401

Southern State College
Springfield, South Dakota 57062

Tennessee

Austin Peay State University
Clarksville, Tennessee 37040

East Tennessee State University
Johnson City, Tennessee 37602

Memphis State University
Memphis, Tennessee 38111

Middle Tennessee State University
Murfreesboro, Tennessee 37130

Tennessee Technological University
Cookeville, Tennessee 38501

Texas

East Texas State University
Commerce, Texas 75429

Midwestern University
Wichita Falls, Texas 76308

North Texas State University
Denton, Texas 76203

Southwest Texas State College
San Marcos, Texas 78666

Stephen F. Austin State College
Nacogdoches, Texas 75962

Sul Ross State College
Alpine, Texas 79831

Texas A & I University
Kingsville, Texas 78363

Texas Woman's University
Denton, Texas 76214

West Texas State University
Canyon, Texas 79015

Utah

College of Southern Utah
Cedar City, Utah 84720

Weber State College
Ogden, Utah 84403

Vermont

Castleton State College
Castleton, Vermont 05735

Johnson State College
Johnson, Vermont 05656

Lyndon State College
Lyndonville, Vermont 05851

Virgin Islands

College of the Virgin Islands
St. Thomas, Virgin Islands 00801

Virginia

Longwood College
Farmville, Virginia 23901

Madison College
Harrisonburg, Virginia 22802

Mary Washington College
Fredericksburg, Virginia 22401

Radford College
Radford, Virginia 24142

Virginia Commonwealth University
Richmond, Virginia 23220

Washington

Central Washington State College
Ellensburg, Washington 98926

Eastern Washington State College
Cheney, Washington 99004

The Evergreen State College
Olympia, Washington 98501

Western Washington State College
Bellingham, Washington 98225

West Virginia

Concord College
Athens, West Virginia 24712

Marshall University
Huntington, West Virginia 25701

Shepherd College
Shepherdstown, West Virginia 25443

West Liberty State College
West Liberty, West Virginia 26074

Wisconsin

Stout State University
Menomonie, Wisconsin 54751

Wisconsin State University
Eau Claire, Wisconsin 54701

Wisconsin State University
La Crosse, Wisconsin 54601

Wisconsin State University
Oshkosh, Wisconsin 54902

Wisconsin State University
Platteville, Wisconsin 53818

Wisconsin State University
River Falls, Wisconsin 54481

Wisconsin State University
Stevens Point, Wisconsin 54481

Wisconsin State University
Superior, Wisconsin 54881

Wisconsin State University
Whitewater, Wisconsin 53190

ASSOCIATE MEMBERS

The California State Colleges
5670 Wilshire Boulevard
Los Angeles, California 90036

Trustees of the State Colleges
in Colorado
219 State Service Building
Denver, Colorado 80203

Board of Trustees of the
Connecticut State Colleges
80 Pratt Street
Hartford, Connecticut 06015

Board of Governors of State
Colleges and Universities
State of Illinois
222 College Street
Springfield, Illinois 62706

Board of Regents
909 Myers Building
Springfield, Illinois 62701

Board of Trustees of the
State Colleges
State of Maryland
93 College Avenue
Annapolis, Maryland 21401

Division of State Colleges
Commonwealth of Massachusetts
50 Franklin Street
Boston, Massachusetts 02110

Minnesota State College Board
Centennial Office Building
St. Paul, Minnesota 55101

University Dean for Four-Year Colleges
State University of New York
Thurlow Terrace
Albany, New York 12201

Board of Regents
State Senior Colleges
State of Texas
1009 Sam Houston Building
Austin, Texas 78701

Vermont State Colleges
481 Main Street
Burlington, Vermont 05401

Board of Regents of State
Colleges, State of Wisconsin
18 East Capitol
Madison, Wisconsin 53702

Appendix B: AASCU Nonmember List

Alabama
Jacksonville State University
Jacksonville, Alabama 36265

California
California Maritime Academy
Vallejo, California 94591

San Francisco State College
San Francisco, California 94132

Colorado
Colorado School of Mines
Golden, Colorado 80401

Fort Lewis College
Durango, Colorado 81303

Florida
University of South Florida
Tampa, Florida 33620

Georgia
Georgia Southwestern College
Americus, Georgia

Georgia State College
Atlanta, Georgia 30303

North Georgia College
Dahlonega, Georgia 30533

West Georgia College
Carrollton, Georgia 30117

Idaho
Lewis-Clark Normal School
Lewiston, Idaho 83501

Massachusetts
Lowell Technological Institute
Lowell, Massachusetts 01854

Southeastern Massachusetts
Technical Institute
North Dartmouth, Massachusetts 02747

Michigan
Michigan Technological University
Houghton, Michigan 49931

Oakland University
Rochester, Michigan 48313

Saginaw Valley College
University Center, Michigan 48710

Western Michigan University
Kalamazoo, Michigan 49001

Montana
Montana College of Mineral Science
and Technology
Butte, Montana 59701

New Mexico
New Mexico Highland University
Las Vegas, New Mexico 87701

New Mexico Institute of Mining
and Technology
Socorro, New Mexico 87801

New York
SUNY Maritime College
Bronx, New York 10465

North Carolina

North Carolina School of the Arts
Winston-Salem, North Carolina 27107

Wilmington College
Wilmington, North Carolina 28403

Ohio

Cleveland State University
Cleveland, Ohio 44115

University of Toledo
Toledo, Ohio 43606

Wright State University
Dayton, Ohio 45431

Oklahoma

East Central State College
Ada, Oklahoma 74821

Murray State College of
Agriculture and Applied Science
Tishomingo, Oklahoma 73460

Northwestern State College
Alva, Oklahoma 73717

Oklahoma College of Liberal Arts
Chickasha, Oklahoma 73018

Panhandle State College
Goodwell, Oklahoma 73939

Southwestern State College
Weatherford, Oklahoma 73096

Oregon

Oregon College of Education
Monmouth, Oregon 97631

Portland State College
Portland, Oregon 97207

South Carolina

Winthrop College
Rock Hill, South Carolina 29733

South Dakota

South Dakota School of Mines
and Technology
Rapid City, South Dakota 57701

Texas

Angelo State College
San Angelo, Texas 76903

Lamar State College of Technology
Beaumont, Texas 77704

Pan American College
Edinburg, Texas 78539

Sam Houston State College
Huntsville, Texas 77341

Tarleton State College
Stephenville, Texas 76401

Virginia

College of William and Mary
Williamsburg, Virginia 23185

Old Dominican College
Norfolk, Virginia 23508

Virginia Military Institute
Lexington, Virginia 24450

West Virginia

Bluefield State College
Bluefield, West Virginia 24703

Fairmont State College
Fairmont, West Virginia 26554

Glenville State College
Glenville, West Virginia 26351

West Virginia Institute of Technology
Montgomery, West Virginia 25136

West Virginia State University
Institute, West Virginia 25112

Appendix C: Weighted National Norms for Freshmen

	All 4-year colleges	Public 4-year colleges	Public universities
Age, in years, as of December 31,1968*			
16 or younger	0.2	0.2	0.1
17	5.7	5.4	4.0
18	78.9	79.4	80.9
19	11.5	10.8	11.6
20	1.4	1.4	1.1
21	0.6	0.6	0.5
Older than 21	1.7	2.2	1.7
Average grade in high school*			
A or A+	5.1	3.1	6.6
A−	10.1	8.0	12.4
B+	18.8	18.4	20.3
B	25.0	26.5	24.5
B−	15.6	16.6	14.6
C+	14.6	15.9	12.6
C	10.3	10.9	8.6
D	0.5	0.5	0.4
Secondary school achievements*			
Elected president of student organization	23.2	20.4	23.4
High rating state music contest	10.7	10.7	12.4
State or regional speech contest	6.2	5.3	7.0
Major part in a play	19.1	18.7	17.4
Varsity letter (sports)	33.0	30.9	30.3
Award in art competition	5.4	4.9	5.1
Edited school paper	13.0	11.4	12.2
Had original writing published	17.8	15.1	17.8
NSF summer program	0.9	0.5	1.1
State or regional science contest	2.6	2.3	3.0
Scholastic honor society	29.8	25.7	35.3
National Merit recognition	8.2	5.1	9.8
Rated academic standards of high school			
Very high	32.0	28.4	34.7
Fairly high	37.0	37.3	36.4

	All 4-year colleges	Public 4-year colleges	Public universities
About average	27.4	30.8	25.2
Probably below average	3.0	2.9	3.0
Definitely below average	0.7	0.7	0.6
Rank in high school class			
Top 1%	5.6	3.9	6.7
Top 10%	23.1	20.1	27.8
Top quarter	29.6	31.8	31.0
Second quarter	26.7	29.3	23.1
Third quarter	12.7	12.8	9.5
Fourth quarter	2.3	2.0	2.0
Highest degree planned*			
None	2.6	2.6	2.4
Associate (or equivalent)	1.8	2.6	1.9
Bachelor's degree (B.A., B.S.)	37.7	40.6	40.4
Master's degree (M.A., M.S.)	38.8	40.1	32.8
Ph.D. or Ed.D.	12.5	9.6	12.6
M.D., D.D.S., or D.V.M.	3.8	2.4	6.5
Ll.B. or J.D.	1.2	0.6	1.9
B.D.	0.2	0.2	0.2
Other	1.3	1.2	1.3
Probable major field of study*			
Agriculture (incl. forestry)	1.2	1.5	2.3
Biological sciences	4.4	4.2	4.1
Business	11.3	12.2	12.4
Education	14.8	19.8	9.4
Engineering	7.8	5.4	12.5
English	5.0	5.1	3.4
Health professions (non-M.D.)	4.0	3.7	5.7
History, political science	8.5	8.5	5.8
Humanities (other)	4.6	4.0	3.6
Fine arts	8.4	7.7	8.7
Mathematics or statistics	5.5	5.8	4.1
Physical sciences	3.0	2.3	3.6
Preprofessional	5.3	3.6	9.3
Psychology, sociology, anthropology	9.9	8.8	7.8
Other fields (technical)	2.3	3.4	1.8
Other fields (nontechnical)	2.1	2.1	3.0
Undecided	1.9	1.9	2.2
Probable career occupation*			
Artist (incl. performer)	5.5	4.5	6.4
Businessman	9.1	8.8	9.9
Clergyman	1.0	0.3	0.2
College teacher	1.3	1.1	1.1
Doctor (M.D. or D.D.S.)	3.5	2.1	5.4
Educator (secondary)	19.6	25.5	11.9
Elementary teacher	12.4	16.7	6.5
Engineer	6.4	4.3	11.7
Farmer or forester	1.1	1.3	1.8

	All 4-year colleges	Public 4-year colleges	Public universities
Health professional (non-M.D.)	3.4	3.8	5.3
Lawyer	3.3	2.2	4.4
Nurse	1.9	1.2	2.7
Research scientist	3.1	2.5	4.1
Other choice	17.5	15.5	16.7
Undecided	11.0	10.1	12.0
Number of applications to other colleges*			
None	41.7	50.7	56.4
One	21.6	22.4	21.1
Two	16.9	14.9	12.1
Three	10.7	7.4	5.9
Four	5.0	2.8	2.5
Five	2.4	1.1	1.2
Six or more	1.7	0.7	0.8
Number of acceptances by other colleges*			
None	36.9	44.7	50.5
One	30.6	30.7	28.4
Two	20.0	17.0	13.8
Three	8.4	5.5	5.0
Four	2.7	1.4	1.5
Five	0.9	0.4	0.5
Six or more	0.5	0.3	0.3
Major influences in deciding to attend this college*			
Parent or other relative	48.3	47.6	46.7
High school teacher or counselor	24.9	25.5	18.2
Friends attending this college	15.5	15.7	16.8
Graduate or other college representative	15.3	12.0	10.3
Counseling or placement service	4.5	4.3	3.8
Athletic program of the college	7.1	6.8	5.1
Other extracurricular activities	5.1	3.9	5.9
Social life of the college	8.1	6.3	9.6
Chance to live away from home	17.4	14.5	19.3
Low cost	20.6	31.7	25.7
Academic reputation of the college	49.0	41.9	52.5
Most students are like me	10.3	8.5	7.0
Religious affiliation	8.7	1.7	1.3
While growing up, I lived			
On a farm	10.1	12.6	9.2
In a small town	22.1	24.9	16.5
In a moderate-size town or city	32.3	31.8	30.9
In a suburb of a large city	21.9	18.0	28.1
In a large city	13.7	12.7	15.3
Region of home state*[1]			
Middle states	31.1	32.3	7.1
New England	6.3	4.4	5.8
North Central	37.7	43.0	49.6
Northwest	2.3	3.4	4.6

	All 4-year colleges	Public 4-year colleges	Public universities
Southern	14.6	8.6	24.8
Western	7.2	8.0	7.7
Foreign	0.8	0.2	0.4
Father's education*			
Grammar school or less	9.7	11.6	8.0
Some high school	16.5	20.2	12.5
High school graduate	29.8	34.1	28.7
Some college	17.9	17.3	19.9
College degree	16.3	11.7	20.2
Postgraduate degree	9.8	5.1	10.7
Mother's education*			
Grammar school or less	5.7	6.5	5.1
Some high school	14.1	17.4	11.2
High school graduate	43.3	47.8	42.6
Some college	19.2	17.0	21.8
College degree	14.7	9.6	16.4
Postgraduate degree	2.9	1.7	2.9
Racial background*			
Caucasian	86.1	84.9	91.6
Negro	8.8	9.8	3.3
American Indian	0.4	0.5	0.5
Oriental	0.8	0.7	0.7
Other	3.9	4.1	3.9
Religious background*			
Protestant	51.6	51.5	56.9
Roman Catholic	33.0	32.7	29.7
Jewish	4.9	4.0	5.6
Other	8.3	9.8	5.4
None	2.1	2.0	2.4
Present religious preference*			
Protestant	46.4	46.7	49.6
Roman Catholic	31.3	31.5	27.6
Jewish	4.2	3.4	5.0
Other	9.2	10.1	6.7
None	9.0	8.3	11.1
Father's occupation*			
Artist (incl. performer)	0.8	0.6	0.9
Businessman	30.3	26.0	33.2
Clergyman	1.1	0.5	0.6
College teacher	0.8	0.5	1.0
Doctor (M.D. or D.D.S.)	2.2	0.8	2.5
Educator (secondary)	2.3	2.4	2.1
Elementary teacher	0.4	0.4	0.3
Engineer	6.7	6.3	8.9
Farmer or forester	6.4	8.2	6.2
Health professional (non-M.D.)	1.0	0.9	1.3
Lawyer	1.3	0.4	1.4

	All 4-year colleges	Public 4-year colleges	Public universities
Military career	1.6	1.2	2.1
Research scientist	0.5	0.3	0.9
Skilled worker	12.3	14.7	11.4
Semiskilled worker	8.8	10.9	6.6
Unskilled worker	4.3	5.4	2.8
Unemployed	1.2	1.5	0.9
Other	17.9	9.3	17.0
Estimated parental income[*2]			
Less than $4,000	7.1	8.4	4.3
$4,000 - $5,999	10.1	12.0	8.1
$6,000 - $7,999	15.1	17.7	13.1
$8,000 - $9,999	16.6	18.2	16.3
$10,000 - $14,999	26.9	27.5	30.0
$15,000 - $19,999	11.4	9.8	13.3
$20,000 - $24,999	5.3	3.5	6.6
$25,000 - $29,999	2.7	1.4	3.0
$30,000 or more	4.9	1.5	5.2
Major sources of financial support during freshman year*			
Personal savings or employment	22.5	27.8	26.1
Parental or family aid	51.9	47.8	59.9
Repayable loan	18.7	18.6	10.1
Scholarship, grant, or other gift	23.2	19.0	15.8
Concern about financing education*			
None	33.0	29.9	34.2
Some concern	57.7	61.0	57.5
Major concern	9.2	9.1	8.3
Objectives considered to be essential or very important*			
Achieve in a performing art	9.7	8.9	8.4
Be an authority in my field	59.7	58.4	60.5
Obtain recognition from peers	38.1	36.7	38.1
Perform or compose music	7.1	6.2	6.4
Be an expert in finance	9.1	8.8	9.6
Be administratively responsible	21.9	20.9	21.9
Be very well off financially	38.0	38.3	41.7
Help others in difficulty	62.6	60.5	56.5
Join the Peace Corps or VISTA	20.5	19.0	17.8
Become an outstanding athlete	12.8	12.1	8.9
Become a community leader	23.0	20.3	21.4
Contribute to scientific theory	10.5	8.6	13.2
Write original works	14.0	12.4	14.2
Not be obligated to people	23.5	24.1	23.3
Create works of art	13.6	12.4	13.9
Keep up with political affairs	54.5	51.5	55.0
Succeed in my own business	41.8	42.3	45.4
Develop a philosophy of life	85.1	83.1	84.0
Students estimate chances are very good that they will*			
Get married while in college	6.4	7.2	7.4
Marry within a year after college	20.4	19.6	19.7

	All 4-year colleges	Public 4-year colleges	Public universities
Obtain average grade of A— or higher	2.4	2.0	3.1
Change major field	15.7	14.7	17.8
Change career choice	16.4	14.8	18.5
Fail one or more courses	2.1	2.2	2.2
Graduate with honors	3.8	3.2	4.3
Be elected to a student office	2.5	1.9	2.2
Join social fraternity or sorority	29.1	25.1	29.2
Author a published article	5.1	4.0	5.0
Be elected to an honor society	2.7	2.0	3.4
Participate in demonstrations	4.7	3.7	3.9
Drop out temporarily	1.0	0.9	0.8
Drop out permanently	0.6	0.5	0.4
Transfer to another college	11.2	11.3	9.6
Study habits (always or usually) during past year			
Turned in assigned work on time	96.9	97.1	97.2
Had trouble concentrating	10.0	9.9	9.5
Kept study place neat	71.1	74.0	69.3
Was too bored to study	6.8	6.4	7.7
Outlined reading assignment	28.5	30.0	25.8
Made careless mistakes on test	11.9	11.4	11.0
Did homework every day	51.7	49.8	49.7
Studied alone	91.5	91.2	92.8
Put off starting homework	19.5	18.1	21.7
Got exam jitters	25.0	24.8	20.1
Fell asleep while studying	3.6	3.4	3.4
Memorized without understanding	6.5	6.6	5.3
Failed to complete assignment	3.2	3.1	2.5
Shared notes with other students	25.3	26.1	23.4
Checked work before submitting	81.5	82.0	80.5
Did work for extra credit	16.3	16.7	16.1
Made up and took own test	8.4	9.0	7.0
Daydreamed while studying	13.4	11.9	14.1
Received lower grade than deserved	2.4	2.4	2.2
Included minor details in notes	28.0	28.2	27.4
Wasted time in bull sessions	12.6	12.3	11.8
Analyzed own mistakes	63.1	62.4	64.2
Read tables, charts carefully	54.6	54.0	55.6
Studied with radio on	20.5	20.9	20.8
Studied with T.V. on	6.0	7.0	6.0
Clarified work with instructor	47.5	47.1	45.8
Agree strongly or somewhat			
Student design of curriculum	89.1	90.2	90.4
Publish all science findings*	53.9	53.2	55.0
Individual cannot change society	31.4	31.8	31.1
College control of student behavior off campus	26.1	25.2	19.6
Benefit of college is monetary*	53.9	58.4	54.4
Base faculty pay on student evaluation*	62.9	63.4	65.7
My beliefs are similar to others	70.2	70.9	69.0
Regulate student publications*	55.8	59.4	51.7
Marijuana should be legalized	18.6	16.2	21.1

	All 4-year colleges	Public 4-year colleges	Public universities
Limit cars to reduce air pollution	45.9	44.7	45.3
Urban problems require much money	51.9	51.8	48.2
Outlaw cigarette advertising	42.4	42.1	39.1
College has right to ban speaker*	30.9	32.1	29.2
Army should be voluntary	37.1	34.9	37.5
Give disadvantaged preferred treatment*	41.0	41.6	38.2
College too lax on student protest*	53.8	54.2	53.1
Percentage of students reporting that during the past year they			
Voted in student election *[3]	78.3	77.5	79.1
Came late to class*	53.6	52.0	52.3
Played a musical instrument*	42.1	39.0	41.3
Studied in the library*[3]	34.5	35.2	33.4
Checked out a library book*[3]	52.9	53.4	50.6
Arranged date for another student*	47.9	47.8	49.7
Overslept and missed a class*	18.1	17.4	16.8
Typed a homework assignment *[3]	21.3	21.3	22.1
Discussed future with parents	40.1	39.9	37.7
Was late with homework assignment*	60.0	59.4	58.7
Argued with teacher in class*	52.0	47.9	55.2
Attended religious service	92.4	92.4	90.9
Protested against Vietnam war	5.1	4.1	3.7
Protested against racial discrimination	8.4	7.1	5.8
Protested against school administration	17.5	16.4	15.8
Did extra reading for class*[3]	11.9	11.5	11.8
Took sleeping pills*	5.5	4.6	5.7
Tutored another student*	50.5	47.5	50.7
Played chess*	40.5	37.9	43.7
Read poetry not required for course	59.8	58.0	58.1
Took a tranquilizing pill*	8.6	7.8	8.4
Discussed religion*[3]	32.4	29.5	30.4
Took vitamins*	59.9	59.4	57.8
Visited art gallery or museum*	72.6	71.0	71.3
Took part in high school political campaign	46.0	43.4	47.3
Took part in other political campaign	13.6	11.1	13.5
Missed school because of illness*[3]	2.8	2.6	2.6
Smoked cigarettes*[3]	13.1	12.0	13.2
Discussed politics*[3]	31.6	27.1	34.0
Drank beer*	49.5	47.7	52.2
Discussed sports*[3]	43.9	42.9	45.0
Asked teacher for advice*[3]	23.5	22.0	21.5
Had vocational counseling*	60.5	62.1	58.4
Stayed up all night*	55.9	55.4	58.7

*Repeated as shown from the 1966 or 1967 surveys.

[1] States have been grouped according to the areas defined by the six regional accrediting associations.

[2] Reported estimate of total income of parental family last year (all sources before taxes).

[3] Frequently only; all other items frequently plus occasionally.

SOURCE: American Council on Education, Office of Research.

Appendix D: Alumni Survey

	State college alumni, %	All alumni, %
A. Highest degree held		
Undergraduate bachelor	70	60
Professional	3	9
Arts and science master	25	21
Doctorate	2	4
B. Field of highest degree		
Education	61	29
C. Number of jobs held now		
None	20	22
One	70	71
More than one	10	7
D. Present job		
Education	53	27
Elementary or secondary school systems	49	24
E. Sex ratio		
Men	52	58
Women	48	42
F. Schools attended		
Public schools	93	81
Community colleges	30	12

	State college alumni, %	All alumni, %
G. Anticipated personal income at designated periods in life		
Period *Anticipated Income:*		
Now *Over $11,000*	18	39
Six years hence *Over $15,000*	40	47
At age 45 *Over $20,000*	33	49
H. Occupational values		
Make a lot of money	25	30
Be helpful to others	75	70
Have stable, secure future	56	44
I. Religious affiliation		
Roman Catholic	16	22
Jewish	2	7
Methodist	17	14
Baptist	15	6
Lutheran	5	7
Congregationalist	1	2
Presbyterian	9	9
Episcopalian	4	7
None	18	15
J. Marital status		
Single, no plans	10	14
Single, plans	1	2
Widowed, divorced, or separated	3	2
Married	85	82
K. Cultural interests (do frequently)		
Read (not necessarily finish) a nonfiction book	39	39
Read (not necessarily finish) a work of "serious fiction"	24	26
Read poetry	9	6
Listen to classical or serious music	29	32
Go to concerts	8	8
Go to plays	11	13
Go to museums or art galleries	11	11

	State college alumni, %	All alumni, %
L. Political and social attitudes		
Political attitudes:		
Conservative Republican	22	21
Liberal Republican	13	21
Conservative Democrat	20	12
Liberal Democrat	22	17
Conservative Independent	11	12
Liberal Independent	10	14
Social attitudes (percent in agreement):		
The protests of college students are a healthy sign for America	40	51
Scientific research is causing the world to change too fast	35	26
This country would be better off if there were less protest and dissatisfaction coming from college campuses	62	52
Because the experts have so much power in our society, ordinary people don't have much of a say in things	39	39
In the long run, current protests of Negroes in the cities will be healthy for America	46	56
The main cause of Negro riots in the cities is white racism	28	35
Negro militancy is needlessly dividing American society into conflicting camps	72	67
The federal government should make a special effort to see that members of minority groups receive a college education	52	56

Things alumni have done and would approve if their children did them:	I have	I would approve	I have	I would approve
Experimented with drugs	3.8	0.2	3.6	1.0
Participated in an antiwar protest	2.0	9.0	4.8	15.0
Participated in a civil rights protest	7.5	21.0	9.0	30.0
Worked full time for a service organization such as the Peace Corps, VISTA, or the American Friends Service Committee	1.6	67.0	2.4	73.0

	State college alumni, %		All alumni, %	
Volunteered to help others (a project to tutor underprivileged students, helping in a mental hospital, etc.)	36.0	87.0	43.0	91.0

M. Student values

Today's students, in contrast to 7 years ago, are more:

Radical	80	75
Politically involved	83	84
Serious	25	27
Moral	3	5
(Much less moral)	(13)	(10)

N. Purposes of college

General education	58.0	71.0
Have a good time	0.8	0.6
Career training	35.0	23.0
Get along with people	7.0	5.0

O. How the alumni perceived the goals of their faculties and administrations (rate as essenti or of great importance)

Develop the inner character of students so that they can make sound, moral choices	22	37
Produce a student who is able to perform his citizenship responsibilities effectively	33	37
Make a good consumer of the student —a person who is elevated culturally, has good taste, and can make good consumer choices	17	17
Produce a well-rounded student, that is, one whose physical, social, moral, intellectual, and esthetic potentialities have all been cultivated	37	50
Prepare student specifically for useful careers	69	54
Assist students to develop objectivity about themselves and their beliefs and hence examine those beliefs critically	25	37
Produce a student who, whatever else may be done to him, has had his intellect cultivated to the maximum	25	32

	State college alumni, %	All alumni, %
Make sure the student is permanently affected (in mind and spirit) by the great ideas of the great minds of history	18	24
Train students in methods of scholarship, and/or scientific research, and/or creative endeavor	32	41
Serve as a center for the dissemination of new ideas that will change the society, whether those ideas are in science, literature, the arts, or politics	15	27
Provide the student with skills, attitudes, contacts, and experiences which maximize the likelihood of his occupying a high status in life and a position of leadership in society	26	30

P. Evaluation of specific aspects of college or university attended (rate as "excellent")

Caliber of classroom teaching	12	18
Curriculum and course offerings	8	22
Facilities and opportunities for research (including library)	13	24
Undergraduate housing	9	16
Caliber of students	6	20
Knowledge and professional standing of faculty	15	29
Personal contacts with faculty	14	15

Q. College as preparation for graduate school and job (rate as "very well" prepared)

Graduate school	21	31
Job	27	27
(Alumni not working)	(25)	(29)

R. Ways college greatly affected alumni

Helped me to learn how to make my own decisions	13	20
Trained me for my present job	44	34
Helped me to learn how to get along with others	18	23
Developed my abilities to think and to express myself	37	41

	State college alumni, %	*All alumni, %*
Gave me a broad knowledge of the arts and sciences	28	35
Prepared me to get ahead in the world	20	19
Expanded my tolerance for people and ideas	25	34
Helped me to form valuable and lasting friendships	24	25
Helped me to formulate the values and goals of my life	15	20
Helped me to learn practical and effective ways of helping people	14	10
Helped prepare me for marriage and family life	4	7

S. Criticisms of college, and courses and activities alumni wished they had more of

Criticisms (rate as "not true at all"):

There was no sense of community or chance for students to participate	45	49
The rules were too restrictive	68	56
There was no chance to do anything of service to the community	54	53
There was no opportunity to understand society or myself	64	62
It was not intellectually stimulating	48	59
The pressure for grades was too intense	50	36

Courses alumni wished they had more of:

Humanities	78	86
Social sciences	44	49
Physical and biological sciences	36	42
Education	64	40

Activities alumni wished they had more of:

Studied more	51	46
Worried more about getting good grades	14	10
Dated more	25	30

T. Financial contribution to alma mater last year

| *None* | 83 | 62 |

	State college alumni, %	All alumni, %
U. Alumni association members		
Yes	31	43
V. I interest students in my college		
Frequently	14	12
Never	30	31
W. College expectation for children		
All boys	92	93
All girls	87	86
At my college	12	18
X. Characteristics of great importance in choice of college for children		
Low cost	18	12
High academic standing	76	82
Training for graduate school	63	61
Y. Emotional attachment to alma mater		
Strongly attached	16	27
Z. Importance of child attending same college		
Important	12	18

Acknowledgments

From the very start, Allan W. Ostar, executive director of AASCU, provided excellent guidance and encouragement. The perceptive comments and suggestions of Clark Kerr and David Riesman have added immeasurably to whatever merit this study may have. I am indebted as well to Howard Bobren and Verne Stadtman of the Carnegie Commission.

Though I take full responsibility for what appears in this report, my sincere thanks go to the following busy people who so patiently and understandingly put up with my questions.

College presidents: Leon Billingsly, Missouri Southern College; Albert W. Brown, State University College at Brockport; George Budd, State College of Pittsburg, Kansas; Evan R. Collins, former president, State University of New York at Albany; John R. Emens, former president, Ball State University; Harold L. Enarson, Cleveland State University; Frank Farner, former president, Federal City College; E. K. Fretwell, State University College at Buffalo; Buell G. Gallagher, former president, City College of the City University of New York; Virgil W. Gillenwater, former president, Trenton State College; John A. Greenlee, California State College at Los Angeles; Robert E. Hill, Chico State College; Leo W. Jenkins, East Carolina University; John W. Maucker, University of Northern Iowa; Kenneth Phillips, Metropolitan State College, Denver; James W. Miller, Western Michigan University; John E. Visser, Kansas State Teachers College.

State and municipal administrators who were particularly helpful: Arthur D. Browne, acting executive director, Board of Higher Education, State of Illinois; Albert Bowker, chancellor, City University of New York; Norman Burns, executive director, North Central Association of Colleges and Secondary Schools; Glenn Dumke, chancellor, California State Colleges; Ralph A. Dungan, chancellor,

Department of Higher Education, State of New Jersey; John D. Millett, chancellor, Ohio Board of Regents; Harry Porter, provost, State University of New York at Albany.

Others to whom thanks are due: Robert Berdahl, professor of political science, San Francisco State College; Robert F. Carbone, assistant to the president, University of Wisconsin; Robert M. Green, Gascoign Bluff, St. Simon Island, Georgia; Fred F. Harcleroad, American College Testing Program; Richard A. Hildreth, coordinator of special program development, Metropolitan State College, Denver; Earl J. McGrath, former director, Institute of Higher Education at Teachers College, Columbia University; Leland L. Medsker, director, Center for Research and Development in Higher Education, University of California; Ernest G. Palola, research sociologist, University of California; William Trombley, education editor, *Los Angeles Times*; C. Robert Pace, professor of education, University of California; J. Dean Parnell, coordinator of administrative services, San Francisco State College; G. Jon Roush, professor of English, Reed College; Alfred D. Sumberg, staff associate, American Association of University Professors; Jesse M. Unruh, former speaker of the assembly, State of California; Paul Woodring, distinguished service professor, Western Washington State College.

Thanks as well must go to the many faculty members and students who so freely gave me their time and valuable insights. I am indebted to Ellen H. Cohen, my secretary, for the accuracy of her guesses in deciphering my tapes. Finally, Mae Lani Sanjek gets special thanks for her help in putting the manuscript in final form.

E. Alden Dunham

July, 1969